REGIONAL GROWTH...
LOCAL REACTION

REGIONAL GROWTH...
LOCAL REACTION

The Enactment and Effects
of Local Growth Control
and Management Measures
in California

Madelyn Glickfeld
Ned Levine

Lincoln Institute of Land Policy
Cambridge, Massachusetts

Copyright © 1992 Lincoln Institute of Land Policy

Library of Congress Cataloging-in-Publication Data

Glickfeld, Madelyn.
       Regional growth—local reaction: the enactment and effects of local growth control and management measures in California / Madelyn Glickfeld, Ned Levine.
       p. cm.
    ISBN 1-55844-119-0: $15.00
       1. Land use—Government policy—California.   2. Cities and towns—California—Growth.   3. Local government—California.   4. California—Economic policy.
    I. Levine, Ned.   II. Title.
    HD266.C2G55   1992
    333.73'17'09794—dc20   91-45456
                                                                                                          CIP

International Standard Book Number: 1-55844-119-0

Printed in the U.S.A. on acid-free text stock.

Lincoln Institute of Land Policy
Cambridge, Massachusetts

Second printing, 1992

CONTENTS

List of Tables and Figures *vii*

Acknowledgements *ix*

Summary *xi*

Chapter 1. Introduction *1*
Growth and the Growth Control Reaction 1
The Political Origins of This Wave of Growth Regulation 5
The Context of Local Growth Controls 7

Chapter 2. Goals and Organization of the Research Project *11*
Survey of Growth Control and Management Measures in
   California Jurisdictions 12
The Survey Instrument 13
Indices of Growth Control and Management Measures 15
Types of Analysis 18
Limitations of the Analysis 18

Chapter 3. Research Findings *21*
The Scope and Distribution of Growth Measures 21
Differences in the Average Number of Measures Enacted by Jurisdictions 21
Jurisdictions without Growth Measures 26
Types of Growth Measures Enacted 27
Other Types of Measures Enacted and Pending 32
Method of Adoption of Different Types of Growth Measures 33
Growth Measures, Local Population Growth, and Local Building Activity 34
Growth Measures and Education, Age, Ethnicity and Income 36
Measures Enacted in Combination: Growth Control Patterns 40
Geographic Differences in the Use of the Six Growth Control Patterns 43
The Role of Time of Enactment of Growth Measures 45
Reasons behind Growth Control Measures as Seen by Responding Jurisdictions 50
Growth Measures and Low-Income Housing 53
Enactment of Growth Measures and Statewide Construction Activity Over Time 57

Chapter 4. A Model of Growth Measure Enactment and Effects *61*
Structure of the Enactment Model 61
The Enactment Model at the Statewide Level: Evaluating Alternatives 63
The Enactment Model in Metropolitan and Non-Metropolitan Areas 65
The Enactment Model at the County Level 69

Structure of the Effects Model   70
Specification of the Effects Model   71
Statewide Results of the Effects Model   73
The Effects Model in Metropolitan and Non-Metropolitan Areas   77
The Effects Model at the County Level   78

Chapter 5.   Discussion and Policy Implications   *79*
Conclusions   79
Reasons for Ineffective Growth Management Measures   80
Refuting Common Perceptions about Growth Controls and Management   82
Broader Policy Implications   82
Three Notable Exceptions for Comprehensive Planning   84

About the Authors   *87*

Appendices   *89*
A.   Survey Questionnaire and Codebook   89
B.   Frequencies of Questionnaire Items   101
C.   Distribution of Measures in California Cities and Counties   125
D.   Map Distribution of All Measures   145
E.   Growth Measure Models for Selected Counties   155

LIST OF TABLES AND FIGURES

Tables

1. Indices of Growth Measures   25
2. Percentage of Jurisdictions with Growth Measures   27
3. Number of Jurisdictions with Growth Measures   28
4. Number of Jurisdictions with Other Growth Measures   32
5. Correlation between Population and Construction Characteristics of Jurisdictions and Number of Growth Measures   35
6. Correlation between Socio-economic Characteristics of Jurisdictions and Number of Growth Measures   36
7. The NIMBY Model: Effects of Expected Variables on Number of Growth Measures   37
8. Effects of Key Socio-economic Characteristics on Number of Growth Measures   39
9. Factor Structure of Growth Measures   41
10. Growth Control Patterns   42
11. Intercorrelation of Growth Control Patterns   43
12. Geographic Distribution of Growth Control Patterns   44
13. Timing of Growth Measure Enactment   46
14. Reasons for Residential Measures   51
15. Reasons for Commercial Measures   51
16. Factor Structure of Reasons for Residential Measures   52
17. Percentage of Jurisdictions with Housing Incentives by Number of Growth Control Measures   53
18. Effects of Housing Incentives on Number of Growth Measures   54
19. Relationship between Low-Income Housing Production and Number of Growth Measures   55
20. Effects of Number of Growth Measures on Low-Income Housing Production   57
21. Stage 1—Enactment Models: Effects of Hypothesized Variables on Annual Number of Growth Measures in State, 1970–1988   64
22. Stage 1—Enactment Models: Effects of Hypothesized Variables on Annual Number of Growth Measures in Metropolitan Regions, 1970–1988   68
23. Stage 2—Effects Models: Effects of Hypothesized Variables on Construction in State, 1973–1988   73
24. Stage 2—Effects Models: Relationship between Hypothesized Variables and Construction in Metropolitan Regions of the State, 1973–1988   76

Figures

1. Population in California, U.S. Census 1860–1990   2
2. Population Increase in California, 1860–1990   2
3. Population Growth Rate in California, 1860–1990   3
4. Enactment of Growth Measures in California, 1967–1988   6
5. Cumulative Percentage of Growth Measures in California, 1967–1988   7
6. Geographical Regions of California   16
7. Metropolitan Regions in California   17
8. California Jurisdictions with One or More Growth Measures   22
9. California Jurisdictions with No Growth Measures   23
10. Number of Growth Measures in California Jurisdictions   23
11. Relationship between Growth Measures and Population Size of Jurisdictions   24
12. Distribution of Growth Measures in California   26
13. Percentage and Frequency of Jurisdictions with Residential Control Measures   28
14. Percentage and Frequency of Jurisdictions with Residential Zoning Measures   29
15. Percentage and Frequency of Jurisdictions with Commercial Measures   29
16. Percentage and Frequency of Jurisdictions with Planning and Other Measures   30
17. Jurisdictions with Urban Limit Lines or Greenbelts   30
18. Jurisdictions with Housing Permit Limitations   31
19. Change in Enactment of Population Control Measures, 1967–1988   47
20. Change in Enactment of Infrastructure Control Measures, 1967–1988   48
21. Change in Enactment of Zoning Control Measures, 1967–1988   48
22. Change in Enactment of Political Control Measures, 1967–1988   49
23. Change in Enactment of Floor Space Control Measures, 1967–1988   49
24. Change in Enactment of General Control Measures, 1967–1988   50
25. Permit Valuation of Construction in California, 1967–1988   58
26. Effect of Non-residential Permit Valuation on Growth Measure Enactment, 1970–1988   59
27. A Hypothetical Model of Growth Controls   62
28. Comparison of Actual and Predicted Number of Growth Measures: From Population Growth and Non-residential Construction Valuation, 1970–1988   66
29. Permit Valuation of Non-residential Construction in Metropolitan Areas, 1973–1988   66
30. Permit Valuation of Residential Construction in Metropolitan Areas, 1973–1988   67

ACKNOWLEDGEMENTS

This research effort was undertaken through the University of California—Los Angeles (UCLA) Extension Public Policy Program. The League of California Cities and the County Supervisors Association of California (CSAC) designed, printed, distributed, and collected the questionnaire. We are especially indebted to Sheryl Patterson at the League and Deanne Baker at CSAC for their support of this project.

Major support for the research came from the Lincoln Institute of Land Policy, along with grants from:

The Urban Land Institute;

The Southern California Gas Company;

The Metropolitan Water District of Southern California; and

The General Telephone Company.

The cooperation and support from among these public, private and research organizations has made it possible to assemble critically important data as a resource to help inform the many groups and organizations that play important roles in addressing the issues arising from rapid growth in California.

In addition, we wish to thank a number of people for their valuable contributions:

1. LeRoy Graymer, Director of the Science and Humanities Division of the UCLA Extension, and Professor Martin Wachs of the Graduate School of Architecture and Urban Planning at UCLA. They were instrumental in finding financial support, in helping us conceptualize the design of the study as well as in providing superb critical feedback;

2. Dr. Ben Chinitz, former research director of the Lincoln Institute of Land Policy; Elizabeth Chant, former director of publications at the Lincoln Institute of Land Policy; Anne Brophy and Mary Beth Martin, project editors at the Lincoln Institute of Land Policy. These individuals were instrumental in making this study a part of the work program of the Institute as well as in disseminating and publishing the product;

3. Earl Plummer of the Southern California Gas Company, who helped us with the initial funding and provided very valuable support;

4. Veronica Tam, our research assistant, who worked so tirelessly to organize the data base and produce files and maps necessary for our analysis;

5. MaBel Collins of the Public Policy Program at UCLA Extension, who has administered our funding;

6. Ben Bartolotto of the Construction Industry Research Board, who provided us with extensive construction data and help in interpreting it; and

7. Jonathan Abrams, who programmed the data entry screen of the questionnaire.

SUMMARY

Policy analysts and private citizens alike are becoming aware that a major change has occurred in local community adoption of growth control and growth management measures. Growth measures that were once atypical are now the norm in many local jurisdictions. To enhance our understanding of the growth control phenomenon in California, and, by comparison, in other parts of the United States, this study documents the scope and distribution of locally enacted growth control and growth management measures in the state. The findings are based on the results of a survey of all local jurisdictions in California to identify the growth measures they had enacted. The main findings are:

1. Enactment of growth control measures in California has increased in the last few years at an accelerating rate in virtually every region of the state. (See page 21.)
2. Populous jurisdictions are more likely to enact growth control measures than are smaller ones; however, other factors are also important. For instance, the average number of measures per jurisdiction also varies by geographic region. (See pages 21–27.)
3. While some types of growth measures are used more often than others (i.e., zoning controls, adequate service requirements), no one type of measure predominates in a majority of jurisdictions. There is no significant difference between the kinds of measures enacted by cities and those enacted by counties, with the exception of urban line limits or greenbelts, which are more often used by counties. (See pages 27–33.)
4. Contrary to previous assumptions about the grassroots initiative base of the growth control movement, the vast majority of local growth measures are passed by local governments through normal public hearing processes, rather than by ballot initiatives. (See pages 33–34.)
5. Surprisingly, there is no relationship between the rate of growth in local jurisdictions and the enactment of growth control measures. (See pages 34–36.)
6. No support was found for the hypothesis that growth control measures come from exclusively white, middle-class communities. Jurisdictions that have passed more measures do tend to have better-educated populations, but these relationships are weak. (See pages 36–39.)
7. Growth measures seem to be enacted in combination with other growth measures in six distinct patterns, which vary both by geographic location and by time of enactment. The most common patterns are infrastructure control, which includes infrastructure requirements for housing or commercial/industrial construction, and zoning control, which includes such measures as height and density limitations and rezoning. Population control, which uses housing permit and population growth limitations, and general control, using a growth management element of the general plan, appear considerably less frequently. The least frequently used patterns are floor space control and political control. (See pages 40–45.)
8. There appears to be a sequencing in the enactment of each growth control pattern. Population control measures appeared earlier, starting in the mid-1970s, followed by infrastructure control measures. Zoning and political control measures are products of the early 1980s, while floor space control and more general approaches have been more common in the late 1980s. (See pages 45–50.)
9. According to the administrators who filled out the questionnaire, three types of reasons for the enactment of growth management and control measures seem to be common: a) urban population growth containment; b) urban infrastructure protection; and c) rural land preservation. Enactment of measures appears to be related to regional environmental, traffic, and infrastructure concerns as perceived by the administrators. Different locales place emphasis on different reasons for enacting growth measures. (See pages 50–52.)
10. Contrary to expectations, jurisdictions that have passed more growth measures have also enacted low-income housing incentives. Despite these incentives, they produce neither a greater nor a lesser amount of low-income housing than jurisdictions without such measures. (See pages 53–56.)

11. Growth measures appear to be a local response to regional growth rather than to growth in any particular city. Models were developed to understand what precipitates enactment of growth measures and to estimate some of the consequences. When examined at the state level, there is a definite relationship between the enactment of growth measures, population growth, and growth in non-residential construction. This relationship also holds at the metropolitan level but starts to break down at the county level, except in the large Los Angeles, Orange, and Riverside Counties, where enactment of growth measures is a specific response to growth within those counties. (See pages 65–70.)

12. Up to the point that we conducted our survey, growth measures do not appear to have reduced construction activity significantly at the state, the county, or the metropolitan level. Whether this is due to the recency of these measures or to some basic defects in their design cannot be determined by our data. (See pages 73–78.)

These findings contradict some common perceptions about the extent and nature of growth measures in California, and, by extension, elsewhere. The final section of this study discusses the survey results in the context of evaluating the effectiveness of the 'de facto' state growth policy in California. The data seem to indicate that the current system of growth control and management, implemented primarily by separate local jurisdictions, is ineffective in addressing the main causes and consequences of growth. We conclude that there is need for a more deliberate regional and state growth policy.

1

INTRODUCTION

The last few years have seen the emergence of a new, populist movement in California aimed at controlling or curtailing growth. This movement, called by various names "Slow Growth," "No Growth," or "Growth Control," is not a statewide movement, but one consisting of a series of networked but independent actions by local groups addressing growth in hundreds of communities throughout the state. Furthermore, these citizen efforts to control growth have markedly changed government attitudes and policies towards growth, even in communities not directly affected by citizen action.

While efforts to control and manage growth have existed in some cities in California for decades, it is only in the last decade that growth control and management systems have been enacted in a substantial majority of California's local jurisdictions. In fact, monitoring the changes in the way that growth is managed in California's cities and counties over the last four years has made us witnesses to the rapid evolution of a new, statewide attitude about land use controls.

Growth and the Growth Control Reaction

Many of the conditions that led to this new California "revolution" in attitudes about land use controls are familiar in other states. Far from being strange and unique in its land use controls practices, California can be thought of as a "bellwether" state—a preview of how local governments in other states will react to high growth in the absence of aggressive national and state growth policy. Three factors seem to have been critical in bringing the growth control reaction: the sheer volume of growth, changing patterns of development, and changing attitudes about growth.

Three factors seem to have been critical in bringing the growth control reaction: the sheer volume of growth, changing patterns of development, and changing attitudes about growth.

First, while California has had nearly continuous high growth rates for the last hundred years, the sheer numbers of people are now enormous. Figure 1 shows the state census population figures from 1860 through 1990, while Figures 2 and 3 display the net increase in persons and the intercensal annual growth rate, respectively. Since 1980, California's population has increased by over six million persons, with a 740,000 – person net increase in population for 1989 alone.[1] The intercensal increase was the largest increase in the state's history and, for that matter, the largest increase for any state in U.S. history.

In the 1980s, only 12.5 percent of the population growth (approximately 75,000 per year) derived from the net increase of migration to the state from other parts of the country. Instead, the vast majority of population growth derived from natural increase and international migration to the state. Twenty-five to 30 percent of the immigration to the entire country through the late 1980s settled in

---

1. California State Department of Finance estimates.

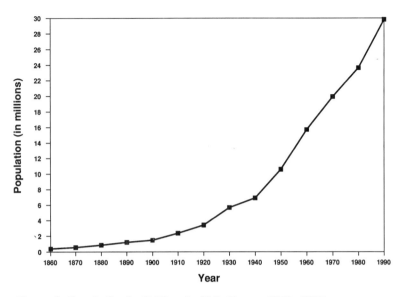

Figure 1. Population in California, U.S. Census 1860–1990

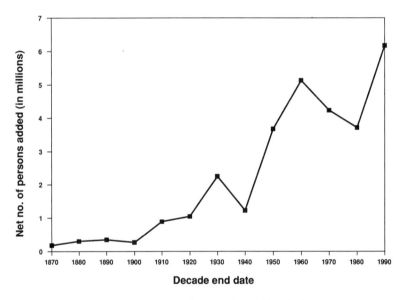

Figure 2. Population Increase in California, 1860–1990

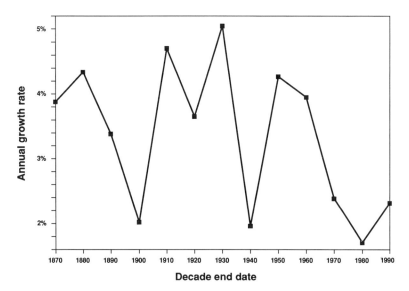

Figure 3. Population Growth Rate in California, 1860–1990

California.[2] This has created an enormous burden for the state. The magnitude of development and infrastructure improvements necessary to supply housing, jobs, schools, and roads is, at the very least, formidable in many areas of the state. The gap between the need for public infrastructure and the ability to provide that infrastructure seems to be getting larger and larger.

Second, there has been a continuation of a national growth pattern with population increasingly spreading into the suburban and exurban areas around major metropoles. This trend has occurred since the last century. However, the 1980s saw a change in the growth pattern as major commercial and industrial development followed housing to the suburbs.[3] These suburban jobs allowed housing to spread even further into the hinterlands and created new cross-cutting, suburb-to-suburb commuter patterns, which strain the capacity of infrastructure not designed for this pattern of development.[4]

Third, while California has experienced growth for a long time, there has been a major change in the attitude of the public and the government about the value and necessity of growth. These changes are contrary to historical attitudes about growth in urban areas. For example, Peterson has argued that cities encourage growth in order to attract investment and employment, as well as to create sufficient revenues necessary to pay for the services required, and they must do so in a competitive economic environment.[5] According to this view, the

2. Center for the Continuing Study of the California Economy, *California Population Characteristics* (Palo Alto, Calif., April 1990).

3. C.K. Orski, "Toward a Policy for Suburban Mobility," in *Urban Traffic Congestion: What Does the Future Hold?* (Washington, D.C.: Institute of Transportation Engineers, 1986); or see Peter Gordon, Ajay Kumar, and Harry W. Richardson, "Congestion, Changing Metropolitan Structure and City Size in the United States," *International Regional Science Review* 1,2 (1989): 45–56.

4. Robert Cervero, *America's Suburban Centers: The Land Use–Transportation Link* (London: Unwin-Hyman, 1989).

5. Paul E. Peterson, *City Limits* (Chicago: University of Chicago Press, 1981).

question is not whether or not cities should grow, but under what conditions. Slow-growing cities are captives of the economic environment and cannot afford to turn down growth. Rapidly growing cities have more choices and can be more selective about the types of investments and land uses they are willing to attract, but they are still constrained by strict competitive and financial restrictions. If they lose their competitive advantage, economic decline may ensue. Thus, according to this view, population growth is a necessity of metropolitan areas and their adjacent hinterlands.

Despite the fact that the behavior of many cities bears out this theory, there is increasingly widespread doubt about the ability of the state to provide the financial and environmental resources for growth and an increasing association of growth with the decrease in the general quality of life in California.[6] Several factors could account for this pivotal change in local attitudes about the benefits and costs of growth. Some cities have distinct locational advantages that allow them to tax and regulate growth without spoiling their investment climate.[7] Many, if not most, California jurisdictions fall in this category. Also, the decline in federal and state funds to subsidize development and the decline of local revenues due to the passage of property tax limitation laws (like Proposition 13 in 1978) has left local governments with limited resources to address the costs associated with growth. Finally, because growth has occurred without concomitant improvements in regional infrastructure, people perceive a decrease in the quality of life, which they link to new development.[8]

Much of the concern about growth in California derives from concerns about increasing traffic congestion. Deakin, for example, has argued that transportation and land use planning in California have never been integrated because transportation planning was conducted at the state and regional levels while land use planning was a local function.[9] This separation has led to inconsistencies between land use and transportation plans. However, as long as transportation agencies stayed within the tradition of providing transportation services on demand and altering transportation plans to meet new land use demands, these inconsistencies were not important. Now, with the current gov-

---

6. See Dominski, Clark, and Relis, "The Bottom Line: Restructuring for Sustainability," Gildea Resource Center Policy Paper, Joan Melcher, ed. (Santa Barbara, Calif.: Community Environmental Council, 1990); Reinhart, "The Desired Land," and Eric Brazil, "Stop!" in *California Tomorrow, Our Changing State*, Vol. 3, nos. 3 & 4 (San Francisco, Fall 1988); Ruane and Gray, *Community Responses to Population Growth and Environmental Stress: A National Inventory of Local Growth Management Strategies* (Washington, D.C.: Population-Environment Balance, Inc., July 1987).

7. Richard Fogelsong, "The Creative Side of Planning: Making the Best of a Bad Bargain," (Harvey Perloff Address, Graduate School of Architecture and Urban Planning, University of California, Los Angeles, 15 February 1990).

8. For example, a 1989 *Los Angeles Times* poll asked Los Angeles County residents about growth and the quality of life in Los Angeles. Although whites differed from blacks and Latinos over whether growth was desirable (a majority of blacks and Latinos favored faster growth), a plurality of all ethnic groups agreed that the quality of life had worsened over the last 15 years. *Los Angeles Times*, 21 June 1989, 1, 25.

9. Elizabeth Deakin, *Land Use and Transportation Planning in Response to Congestion: A Review and Critique* (68th Annual Meeting of the Transportation Research Board, 22–26 January 1989), 1.

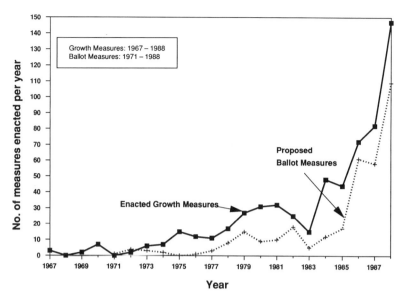

All of these factors have led to dramatic increases in the enactment of local growth controls and growth management measures in California in the last half of the 1980s.

Figure 4. Enactment of Growth Measures in California, 1967–1988
Note: Excludes 29.5 percent of total measures for which no date of enactment was reported.

ernment fiscal crisis, "shrinking revenues, escalating costs and concerns about social and environmental impacts have combined to constrain state highway building. Consequently, it is no longer possible to rely on state and regional transportation agencies to build their way out of congestion problems and local governments are having to shoulder the greater responsibility for transportation."[10] The local response to these conditions has typically been impact fees, transportation demand management programs, and growth management approaches rather than major public financing of road construction.

All of these factors have led to dramatic increases in the enactment of local growth controls and growth management measures in California in the last half of the 1980s. Figure 4 displays the number of individual growth control or management measures enacted each year between 1967 and 1988, based on our survey of statewide measures (to be shortly discussed).[11] Figure 5 shows the cumulative percentage of growth control measures enacted between 1967 and 1988; as shown, 50 percent of the measures have been enacted since the end of 1984. In total, by the end of 1988, 907 local growth control or management measures had been enacted in the state. The rapid rise in the enactment of measures in the last few years has been almost epidemic. This recent, rapid escalation of enactment of local growth controls is a major socio-political phenomenon, comparable in its effects with the

10. Deakin, *Land Use and Transportation,* Abstract.

11. We were able to obtain the date of enactment for 70.4 percent of the 907 measures. It was not requested for measures involving a growth control element in the general plan (n=51). The respondents did not provide this data for the remaining missing dates (n=217). Figures 4 and 5 display those measures for which the date of enactment was known. While bias may have been introduced in the time series by not including 29.6 percent of the measures for which the date is not known, the close fit with ballot initiatives (see Figure 4) suggests that any bias is not large.

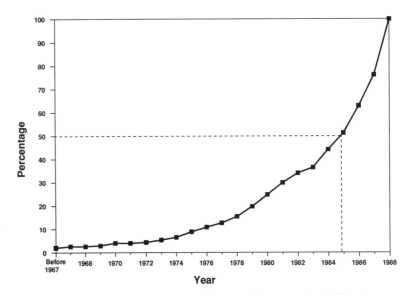

Figure 5. Cumulative Percentage of Growth Measures in California, 1967–1988
Note: Excludes 29.5 percent of total measures for which no date of enactment was reported.

enactment of Proposition 13 in the late 1970s. Since many of the conditions that gave rise to this major change in local government policy exist now, or will exist in the future in other states, there is a good possibility that other states will follow the California experience in local growth management practice.

The Political Origins of This Wave of Growth Regulation

A major trigger of the latest rise in land use controls in California was a wave of land use–related ballot measures that started about 1986. While a total of 357 land use planning measures were placed on local ballots between 1971 and 1989, over 70 percent of those measures were placed on the ballot in the three years between 1986 and 1989. In 1988 alone, 109 measures were placed on the local ballot.[12] The passage rate of land use ballot measures has been startlingly high over the last four years, but even when land use ballot measures didn't pass, they had major effects on both local politics and local land use regulation. There has been a substantial amount of networking between grassroots activists in different parts of the state. These activists consulted with the same land use experts to draw up initiatives. It is not mere coincidence that successful city initiatives in northern California started showing up in identical wording on city ballots in southern California.

In 1988, measures affecting the growth rate in three of the most populous counties in southern California—San Diego, Riverside, and Orange Counties—were placed on the ballot and, if passed, would have affected a majority of the developable land left in southern Cali-

12. California Association of Realtors, "Matrix of Land Use Planning Measures, 1971–1989," Los Angeles, September 1989.

fornia. The development community responded with large-scale campaigns against all of these measures and none of the measures passed. However, despite the failure of these measures, all three counties, plus neighboring San Bernardino County, have since adopted substantial changes in local growth policy and regulation. This is indicative of a major underlying trend—that more growth control and growth management programs have actually been enacted by local government in the wake of the citizens' movement than have been enacted through the ballot itself.

Many local environmentalists have ridden the coattails of this grassroots ballot box planning movement into office and have made very marked changes in local government growth policy.

Many local environmentalists have ridden the coattails of this grassroots ballot box planning movement into office and have made very marked changes in local government growth policy. Some of the elections have been dramatic. For example, in an underfinanced campaign, a virtual unknown, Ruth Galanter, defeated the President of the Los Angeles City Council in a contest primarily dominated by growth and development issues. This election was won in the aftermath of a successful initiative campaign, Proposition U, which cut commercial building heights near residential neighborhoods all over the city. Political events such as these have occurred throughout California and, along with the success of ballot measures, have prompted established local officials who used to favor growth to rethink their positions. As a result, there are a lot of "born again" growth control officials in California.

The Context of Local Growth Controls

It would be a mistake to suggest that this recent wave of local growth management legislation is the sole determinant of how land is used. Instead, the recent rise in the number of locally enacted growth controls must be viewed in the context of a very elaborate and varied array of factors that directly or indirectly control or influence the use of land. Both the state and the federal government make land policy through the ownership of land, through legislation regulating the use of land, through allocation of funding for public works, and through tax policy. Federal and state governments own vast tracts of land and either inhibit or encourage growth through the use of that land.[13] Federal legislation greatly influences the use of land. Examples of federal legislation that directly affect the use of land include the National Environmental Policy Act,[14] which requires the Federal government to assess the environmental impacts of any project initiated by a federal agency or on federal lands, the Water Pollution Control Act,[15] which requires that development not pollute water, either through inadequate sewage treatment facilities or through inadequate control of urban runoff, and the Endangered Species Act,[16] which protects the habitat of endangered species from development.

---

13. For example, acquisition of land for wilderness preservation could discourage growth in the vicinity; conversely, expansion of a military base could be an important incentive for growth in adjoining areas.

14. The National Environmental Policy Act (NEPA) 42 U.S.C.A. Section 4332.

15. Federal Water Pollution Control Act 33 U.S.C.A. 1362 (7).

16. Endangered Species Act 16 U.S.C.A. Section 1531 et seq.

California has detailed legislation that requires each local government to adopt and update general plans for growth and then implement the adopted plans. Other examples of California legislation that profoundly affects the use of land include the Williamson Act, which provides for preferential assessment of land in agricultural preserves,[17] and the California Environmental Quality Act,[18] which requires that every development project requiring discretionary approval by a public agency be analyzed for environmental impacts.

The fiscal decisions made by both the state and federal government as to where, when, and how much money will be spent for infrastructure are important in determining the location and magnitude of growth. Federal and state dollars spent on highways, rapid transit, water pollution control facilities and water development projects are critical in determining how much growth can occur in a given area and whether development will be adequately served. The marked decline in federal and state funding of infrastructure, with a resultant negative impact associated with growth, may be the single most important reason why local attitudes about growth have become more negative.

Federal and state tax policy also has a profound effect on the use of land. For example, in California, there is a growing concern that the increasing reliance of local government on sales tax revenue in the post-Proposition 13 era and the state system of "point-of-sale" distribution of sales tax revenues may be responsible for the "fiscalization" of the local land use decision-making process.[19] That is, "fiscalization" of the land use planning process occurs when the need for local revenue becomes a primary factor in the land use planning process, when local governments choose land uses according to their tax revenue potential, or when local governments try to locate tax-generating facilities where their community will gain the most fiscal benefit. Under such conditions, surrounding communities frequently absorb the costs (i.e., traffic congestion, air pollution). When the land use decision-making process is driven mainly by fiscal criteria, rather than by the full range of social, economic, and environmental values, local dissatisfaction with the planning process may result, triggering efforts to control growth further.

We are barely touching on the array of other mechanisms that influence land use; California does have some of the most sophisticated and stringent local planning requirements in the country. However, the rapid rise in growth control measures is occurring despite the existence of all these other mechanisms to control growth. These measures may indeed fill some gaps that other current governmental land ownership, regulation, and fiscal and tax policy do not address. For instance, California does not require that locally adopted plans conform to some greater overall regional and state substantive policy. The state does not have clear rules for keeping jurisdictions from starting "land

17. Williamson Act (California Land Conservation Act of 1965), California Government Code Sections 51200 – 51295.

18. California Environmental Quality Act (CEQA), California Public Resources Code Sections 21000 et seq.

19. Dean Misczynski, "The Fiscalization of Land Use," in John Eirlin, ed., *California Policy Choices, Vol. III* (Los Angeles: University of Southern California, 1986), 73.

use border wars" by trying to place undesirable uses where neighboring cities absorb the environmental impact while the governing jurisdiction obtains the revenue. The state does not have clear rules for siting of many necessary but undesirable regional facilities such as prisons or incineration plants. Finally, the state does not have a policy or plan to insure that state capital investments are made in a manner to support local development plans or to conform to a set of statewide priorities about where, when, and how investments in infrastructure to support growth ought to be located. The enactment of local growth controls appears, in part, to be a response to these gaps in state policy.

The enactment of local growth controls appears, in part, to be a response to these gaps in state policy.

2

GOALS AND ORGANIZATION OF THE RESEARCH PROJECT

While it has been the common thinking in California that local growth control and growth management programs extended well beyond those highly publicized measures on the ballot, there has been no organized information on how many jurisdictions have enacted growth management and growth control programs, what types of measures were enacted, and where they were enacted.[20] The basic goal of our research project was the creation of a statewide atlas documenting the scope and distribution of different kinds of growth control and growth management measures currently enacted in local jurisdictions throughout California. Our research combines this atlas with other information about statewide and local characteristics to explain when, how, why, and under what conditions local growth control and management measures have been enacted. While the research does not evaluate how any particular growth regulation is implemented in a particular jurisdiction, it does present a picture of the de facto state and regional growth policy as the sum of enacted local growth policies in a state that has no formal state or regional growth policies. By understanding this de facto growth policy, policymakers can decide whether or not this represents the preferred future for California. California's experience with this de facto policy is instructive for other states that do not have a comprehensive statewide or regional land use policy.

This research is designed to make the atlas of local growth regulation a building block for future research on a number of topics, including:

- Evaluating the effectiveness and side effects of implementing particular types of growth regulation in particular communities and analyzing how implementation of growth measures changes over time;

California's experience with this de facto policy is instructive for other states that do not have a comprehensive statewide or regional land use policy.

---

20. While there has been no overall study of growth controls in all of California's local jurisdictions, Deakin conducted a review of empirical research on particular growth management programs in specific California jurisdictions in 1988 (Elizabeth Deakin, "Growth Controls and Growth Management: A Summary and Review of Empirical Research," prepared for UCLA Extension Public Policy Program Conference, "The Growth Controversy in California: Searching for Common Ground," Redondo Beach, Calif., June 1988). She found that there were very few studies of growth management programs in particular jurisdictions with results that were obtained by acceptable scientific methods and that could be considered unbiased scientific evaluations of those programs. Since her review, several researchers have begun to do additional empirical work evaluating the intent and effects of growth management programs in California jurisdictions (e.g. Dr. John Landis at University of California, Berkeley, Dr. Harvey Molotch at University of California, Santa Barbara and Dr. Max Neiman at the University of California, Riverside), but none of that work is completed and published at this time.

- Understanding the basic demographic, social, political, and economic differences between communities that enact growth regulation and those that do not; and
- Understanding the subregional and regional implications of the combined local growth regulations enacted within constituent jurisdictions.

Survey of Growth Control and Management Measures in California Jurisdictions

The main source of information was a survey of growth management and growth control measures in all of California's local jurisdictions, undertaken jointly by the League of California Cities (the "League") and the County Supervisors Association of California (CSAC). The survey instrument was designed by the League with the assistance of the authors. In the fall of 1988, the survey instrument was sent to each of the state's 57 counties and 451 cities, addressed to city managers in cities and county administrative officers in counties. CSAC followed up its initial mailing with telephone calls to all nonresponding counties. The League followed up with a second mailing in February, 1989. The research team subsequently followed up with telephone surveys to insure the inclusion of key large cities.

The survey asked respondents to identify the types of growth controls or management approaches that were currently in force in their jurisdictions. It was necessary to survey both counties and incorporated cities because, in California, the power to regulate land use is delegated to cities for the area within their corporate boundaries and to counties for all unincorporated areas outside cities.[21]

The response rate by local jurisdictions was very high. All fifty-seven counties responded to the survey[22] as did 386 of 451 cities, for an overall response rate of 87 percent.[23] The responding jurisdictions include 95.6 percent of the 1989 state population and 99.3 percent of its land area.[24] Thus, given the response to this survey, it can be regarded as an inventory of local growth measures in California's local jurisdictions through the end of 1988.

---

21. Counties have no regulatory control of land use within city boundaries. Cities have certain obligations to give input to counties on development within a designated "sphere of influence" around the city within which land may be annexed to the city.

22. While California has fifty-eight counties, the City and County of San Francisco is counted in our data base only as a city.

23. All but one of the non-responding cities are small. More than 80 percent have populations smaller than 30,000. There is only one city (Fullerton) with a population greater than 100,000 persons. The geographical distribution of the non-responding cities is similar to the distribution for those jurisdictions that responded, except that there are slightly more non-responding cities in the southern inland area of the state. We do not believe that the survey results have been skewed by not including non-responding cities.

24. Population data from the California Department of Finance. Land area data from the California Office of Planning and Research and the U.S. Census Bureau.

The Survey Instrument

Appendix A presents the questionnaire and the list of coding instructions. The survey results were coded into a *dBase IV* file and cross-checked against other available data and another survey of local government growth management activities.[25] Appendix B presents the frequencies of individual items on the questionnaire.

The survey was aimed primarily at documenting growth control or growth management measures, which we shall refer to collectively as "growth measures." Different jurisdictions have defined "growth management" and "growth control" in different ways. In our cover letter to the California jurisdictions that were surveyed (see Appendix A), we defined growth control and growth management measures as those restricting the rate, intensity, type, and distribution of development in the jurisdiction. The diversity of measures that fall under this definition ranges from attempts to restrict the volume or rate of residential or commercial construction and tightening up zoning to prevent land zoned for residential purposes from becoming a commercial area, to enacting zoning restrictions to prevent agricultural or open space from being built on altogether and instituting urban limit lines. A range of political measures has also been adopted that require, for example, city council supermajorities to increase zoning densities, or even, in a few rare cases, to require voter approval for increased zoning densities.

The survey questions sought information about types of growth control and management approaches known to exist commonly or that had been placed on the ballot in local jurisdictions.[26] In our instructions to respondents, we defined measures as those that control the rate, intensity, type and distribution of development within the jurisdiction. We asked whether the measure was adopted as an ordinance by the governing body or through the initiative ballot process. It should be stressed that we counted the number of *types* of measures enacted in a jurisdiction, not the number of separate ordinances. It is possible that one ordinance could cover several types of measures. Within the survey, fourteen specific types of growth measures adopted at the local government level are identified (question numbers in parentheses):

1. **Population growth caps**: Measures that establish a population growth limit or restrict the level of population growth for a given time period (Q9);[27]
2. **Housing permit limitations**: Measures that restrict the total number of residential building permits in a given time period (Q10);

25. Survey research conducted by Dr. Max Neiman, Department of Political Science, University of California at Riverside. Professor Neiman did a more detailed survey of growth management approaches that he sent to all cities in southern California (no counties). Our initial comparison of results suggests consistent data and findings from our two respective surveys. *dBase IV* is a trademark of Borland International.

26. This typology was created from the experience of the authors in monitoring ballot measures and from a typological analysis proposed by Elizabeth Deakin. See Glickfeld, Graymer, and Morrison, "Trends in Local Growth Control Ballot Measures in California," UCLA *Journal of Environmental Law and Policy,* (1987):6:2; and see Deakin, "Growth Controls and Growth Management."

27. (Q#) is the question number in the survey instrument, which is referenced throughout the text and in Appendices A and B.

3. **Residential infrastructure requirements**: Measures that specifically require adequate service levels (i.e., road capacity or traffic congestion) or service capacity (i.e., water or sewer service capacity) prior to or as a condition of residential development approval (Q11);

4. **Residential downzoning**: Measures to reduce the permitted residential density by general plan amendment or ordinance (Q12A);

5. **Required voter approval for upzoning**: Measures to require that general plan and zoning ordinance amendments that allow increased residential densities be submitted to the voters in a ballot measure (Q12B);

6. **Required council supermajority for upzoning**: Measures to require that some or all general plan and zoning ordinance amendments that allow increased residential densities be approved by a greater than simple majority of the governing board of the local jurisdiction (Q12C);

7. **Rezone residential land to a less intense use**: Measures to rezone or redesignate land previously zoned for residential use to agriculture, open space, or other less intense uses (Q12D);

8. **Commercial square footage limitations**: Measures to restrict the amount of square footage of commercial structures that can be built within a given time frame (Q17A);

9. **Industrial square footage limitations**: Measures to restrict the amount of square footage of industrial structures that can be built within a given time frame (Q17B);

10. **Commercial/industrial infrastructure requirements**: Measures that specifically require adequate service levels (e.g., road capacity) or service capacity (e.g., water or sewer service) prior to, or as a condition of, commercial or industrial development approval (Q18);

11. **Rezone commercial/industrial land to a less intense use**: Measures to rezone or redesignate land previously zoned for commercial use to residential, agriculture, open space or other less intense uses (Q19);

12. **Commercial building height limitations**: Measures enacted within the last five years to restrict the permitted height of commercial buildings (Q20);

13. **Growth management element of the general plan**: A comprehensive plan to address growth issues within the context of the general plan (Q8F); and

14. **Urban limit line or greenbelt**: A limit, inside of and other than the boundaries of the jurisdiction, beyond which residential, commercial, or industrial development is not currently permitted (Q25).

In addition, some other existing or pending measures that did not fit the general categories were noted. Since measures on the ballot often addressed residential or commercial growth issues separately, that same approach was taken in the survey.

The survey also inquired about several issues concerning the context in which the measures were adopted:

- Perceived growth demand and development character;
- Currency and status of general planning efforts;

- Whether the measures were adopted by initiative ballot measure or through local ordinance;
- Perceived purpose of the growth measure;
- Perceived impacts of the growth measure;
- Whether residential growth measures exempted low or moderate income housing;
- Local jurisdiction incentives for low or moderate income housing;
- Local jurisdiction enactment of jobs-housing balance or jobs-housing linkage policies or programs; and
- Documenting studies for either monitoring or formally evaluating the effects of the growth management measures.

In order to understand fully the conditions surrounding the enactment of these measures, the survey results were analyzed in the context of information about the location of the jurisdiction, the current population and population growth rate, some socio-economic indices of the population, and changes in the rates of construction and construction valuation.[28]

Indices of Growth Control and Management Measures

Six indices were developed to measure the extent of growth control regulation:

1. Whether the jurisdiction passed one or more measures (and whether the jurisdiction did not pass any measures). This was done in order to understand whether jurisdictions were formally committed to growth management or control;

2. A *count* of the total number of different types of measures passed by a jurisdiction and the *average* number of measures passed. This was conducted to understand the relative importance jurisdictions placed on growth management;

3. Whether the jurisdiction passed *each* of fourteen different types of measures. This index was used to understand geographical patterns of enactment of particular approaches;

4. A *scale* of the number of different types of measures passed, which was used to assess correlates at the jurisdiction level of socio-economic characteristics, low-income housing incentives, the level of low-income housing need, and the level of low-income housing production;

5. A grouping of different patterns of measures based on a *factor analysis* of the fourteen different types of measures. This was conducted to assess patterns of enactment and a time analysis of the enactment pattern; and

6. The number of measures passed *each year* across all jurisdictions between 1967 and 1988. This index was used to examine the relationship over time between growth measures, population growth, and construction activity.

---

28. Population and household data for 1979, 1984, and 1988 were collected from the California Department of Finance. Construction valuation and permit data for 1967 through 1988 are from the Construction Industry Research Board, Burbank, Calif.

Figure 6. Geographical Regions of California

We analyzed these indices for the state as a whole, for specific geographic regions (Figure 6) and for four major metropolitan areas: San Diego, San Francisco Bay Area, Los Angeles metropolitan area, and the emerging Stockton-Sacramento metropolitan area (Figure 7), as well as for counties combined with their constituent cities and, where possible, individual jurisdictions.

These indices do not calibrate the strength or intensity of a measure; that would have been too complicated an exercise, given the nuances and complexities of individual ordinances. For example, the administrator who filled out the questionnaire could have been asked to rate the intensity of the measure (on a seven-point scale, for example). We did not ask this on the grounds that the meaning of different scale points would still have been unclear (e.g., would a "4" in one jurisdiction be definitely stronger than a "3" in another jurisdiction?).

The approach taken emphasized precision in measuring *extensiveness,* but allowed imprecision with respect to intensity. If one were ideally scaling growth measures, one would do both. The scales constructed in this study are a reasonable approximation. The study indexes the number of different types of measures that a jurisdiction enacts. Thus, the analysis assumes that a jurisdiction that has passed two different types of measures has intervened in more growth issues than a jurisdiction that has passed only one, and certainly more than a jurisdiction that hasn't passed any measures. For example, a local jurisdiction enacting an urban limit line as its only formal growth regulation is less likely to restrict development inside that urban limit line than a city that has an urban limit line, an infrastructure adequacy re-

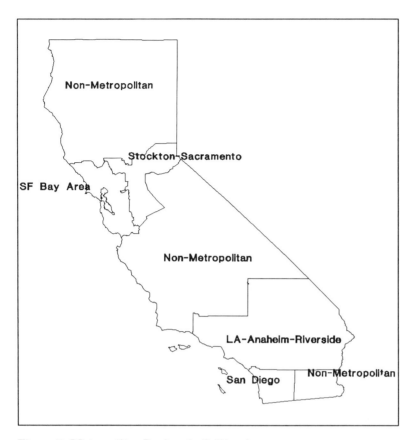

Figure 7. Metropolitan Regions in California

quirement, an annual cap on residential building permits, and a commercial height limitation. Our analysis does not count up the number of ordinances passed in a given jurisdiction, but the number of different *types* of growth measures enacted in those ordinances.[29]

A completely different index was used for the analysis of construction activity between 1967 and 1988, however: the number of types of measures passed by *all* jurisdictions for a given year. Thus, for the statewide analysis, this is the number of types of measures passed by all California jurisdictions in that year. For the metropolitan analysis, this is the number of types of measures passed by all jurisdictions within the metropolitan area for a given year. While it is true, in theory, that this time series index could be even more precise by scaling it for intensity as well as scope, we seriously doubt the predictability of the measure would improve any by doing so.

---

29. The analysis loses precision in assigning a binomial value to the strength of association ('0' for not passing a measure and '1' for passing a measure, whatever the level of intensity). A simple statistical experiment will show that when one collapses a multi-point scale into a binomial one, the correlation will decrease since the within-category variance increases relative to the between-category variance. However, if there is an association between the scale and some external variable (e.g., the association between growth control enactment and the production of affordable housing), the correlation will still hold up, though at a reduced level of association. When one adds individual items (e.g., enactment of a housing cap + enactment of infrastructure controls +, etc.), however, the combined scale increases its sensitivity again.

Types of Analysis

We conducted eight different types of analysis:

1. A descriptive analysis of the distribution and extent of measures. We conducted this for the state as a whole, for city-county combinations, for major metropolitan and non-metropolitan areas, and for specific geographical regions. We present this analysis both as tables and as maps;
2. A correlation and regression analysis comparing the population and building growth characteristics and the socio-economic characteristics of jurisdictions with the number of growth measures enacted;
3. A factor analysis of the different types of measures, to detect combinations of measures that are likely to be enacted together in the same jurisdiction;
4. A time series analysis of the enactment pattern of these combinations, to detect sequencing of enactment;
5. A descriptive and factor analysis of the perceived reasons for the enactment of these measures;
6. A descriptive and regression analysis of the relation between the number of growth measures enacted and incentives toward, need for, and production of, low-income housing;
7. A time series analysis of trends in population growth and construction activity and their effects on the enactment of growth measures; and
8. A time series analysis of the effect of growth measure enactment on subsequent construction activity.

Limitations of the Analysis

There are certain limitations of this analysis that arise from the design of the survey. The first limitation may result from confusion of respondents over the interpretation of a growth management or control measure. In our instructions, we defined growth measures as those that control the rate, intensity, type, and distribution of development within the jurisdiction, whether adopted as an ordinance by the governing body or enacted through the initiative ballot process. It is possible that not all respondents used the concept in the same way. For example, some respondents may have understood growth measures as only those resulting from ballot initiatives. Other respondents with negative views of growth control may have declined to label regulation undertaken by their jurisdictions as such. One respondent remarked that the measures asked about were not "growth control devices, they were just good planning." In these cases, our documentation of the extent of growth control would be understated. On the other hand, it is possible that there is an overestimation of the extent of growth regulation through the interpretation of a rather minor and routine regulation as actually representing a growth control or management measure. In other words, there are potential sources of both underestimation and overestimation of the extent of growth control.

Our study did not attempt to inventory approaches that may have indirect effects on the rate and volume of growth in a particular jurisdiction, such as development impact fees, temporary moratoria, or lengthy review procedures. The study is focused on measuring the explicit extent of permanent, formally adopted growth control or management measures. While we acknowledge that omission of these indirect factors may have also led us to underestimate the full extent of local growth controls in California jurisdictions, our focus was on the formal means. Further research should be conducted on these indirect means.[30]

Another major limitation of the research is our inability to say anything about the specific context in which the measures were enacted, how the measures were implemented once enacted, and how implementation changed over time in any particular jurisdiction. Neither the context nor the strength of effect of a measure can be obtained by simply noting its enactment. Also, our research hinges on the reliability of the survey results, which depend on the knowledge of the single respondent chosen to fill out the survey.[31] The very terms "growth control" and "growth management" are value-laden, and reactions to the terms could have affected the way in which respondents addressed the questionnaire.

Some respondents who identified measures enacted in their jurisdiction did not answer detailed questions about the conditions of enactment of those measures or the purposes or impacts of those measures. There is a 20 to 30 percent non-response rate on subsequent questions about the method of adoption, area of application, and time of enactment of measures. This could possibly bias the results if the non-respondents to those questions are different from those responding. Where possible, we have attempted to evaluate the effect of this bias and have discussed it with the results.

---

30. While ad hoc actions are used by local governments to manage growth, without formalizing the process jurisdictions expose themselves to legal action. Local governments that consistently turn down development in the absence of formal growth controls are taken to court. Most local governments have enacted some type of permanent measures to guide case-by-case decisions.

31. It should be recognized that the survey asks for a broad range of information on general planning, specific growth controls, and housing activities of the jurisdiction. Particularly in large jurisdictions, respondents could be more specialized and, therefore, the reliability of responses to the broad array of questions could vary. In addition, the survey asks for the opinion of the respondent in several instances, and that opinion may not be representative of general opinion in the government of the jurisdiction. Also, the respondents to the survey were typically administrative or planning personnel familiar with growth-related planning issues, not staff experts on local jurisdiction housing activities. This may have led to an understatement of housing incentives, particularly in larger jurisdictions where roles and responsibilities are more specialized.

3

RESEARCH FINDINGS

The Scope and Distribution of Growth Measures

Growth control or management measures are applied in one form or another in the vast majority of California's local jurisdictions. About 72 percent of all responding local jurisdictions reported that they had at least one growth measure enacted;[32] this breaks down into 71 percent of all cities and 77 percent of all counties. In total, our survey documented 907 different growth control or management measures that were "on the books" in 443 local California jurisdictions through the first quarter of 1989.

Figure 8 maps the geographic distribution of jurisdictions with *one or more* measures throughout California, while Figure 9 maps the geographic distribution of jurisdictions that have enacted *no* growth measures. While jurisdictions with growth measures outnumber jurisdictions without measures by a factor of three to one, it is clear that both kinds of jurisdictions are scattered throughout the state, and many jurisdictions with measures directly adjoin jurisdictions without any growth controls. There are only slight variations between the distribution of jurisdictions without measures in different geographic areas. Non-metropolitan and rural areas are more likely than metropolitan areas *not* to have any growth control or management measures.

Growth control or management measures are applied in one form or another in the vast majority of California's local jurisdictions.

Differences in the Average Number of Measures Enacted by Jurisdictions

The number of types of measures enacted was counted for each jurisdiction. Appendix C presents the distribution of measures for all cities and counties in California. These data were analyzed because, as argued earlier, it is likely that the effects of enacting a greater variety of types of growth controls may be cumulative. Figure 10 shows the distribution of California jurisdictions according to the number of growth measures enacted. About 49 percent of all responding local jurisdictions have enacted or have pending at least two types of growth measures. About 19 percent of responding local jurisdictions have enacted four or more types of growth measures.

The average number of types of measures enacted in a local jurisdiction in California is 1.9. However, this average varies significantly in relation to the current population size of the jurisdiction, as shown in Figure 11. As the population size increases, so does the average number of types of measures enacted. Most of the large cities in the state have a sizeable number of measures: Los Angeles—8; San

Non-metropolitan and rural areas are more likely than metropolitan areas not *to have any growth control or management measures.*

---

32. On one measure, whether the jurisdiction had a growth management element in its general plan, the question asked was whether it had been enacted it or was pending. On all other measures, however, the questions only asked about enacted measures.

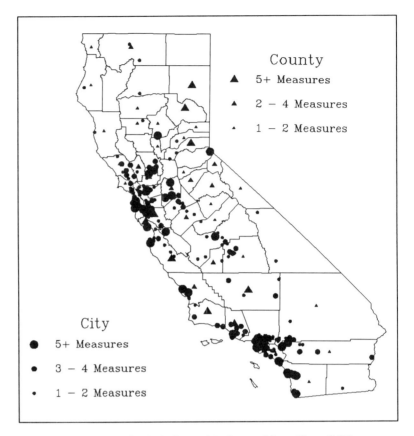

Figure 8. California Jurisdictions with One or More Growth Measures

More populous jurisdictions are more likely to have enacted growth control measures than less populous ones.

Diego—4; San Jose—9; San Francisco—7; Fresno—7; Riverside—6; and the unincorporated areas of Los Angeles County—5.

More populous jurisdictions are more likely to have enacted growth control measures than less populous ones. The correlation between the number of types of growth measures passed by a jurisdiction and its 1988 population was 0.24, which is statistically significant.[33] This significant relationship holds for most of the individual growth measures as well. Larger jurisdictions are more likely to have adopted or have pending a general plan growth management element (r=0.24), to have reduced residential density (r=0.15), and to have enacted other growth control measures (r=0.21).

However, exceptions to these general findings exist among both heavily and lightly settled jurisdictions. For example, two smaller jurisdictions outside of metropolitan areas, San Juan Bautista and San Luis Obispo, have enacted nine of the fourteen types of measures; each had one additional measure pending at the time of the survey.

---

33. The correlations used were Pearson Product-Moment correlations, specified by *r*. They indicate the direction and degree of association with +1.00 indicating a perfect positive association, –1.00 indicating a perfect negative association and 0.00 indicating no relationship. With a sample size of 443 jurisdictions, as a rough approximation one can take an *r* of plus or minus 0.09 as indicating a significant difference from no association (i.e., 0). This assumes a simple random sample from a larger population. However, virtually any correlation is significantly different from zero, given that we have sampled a high proportion of California's jurisdictions.

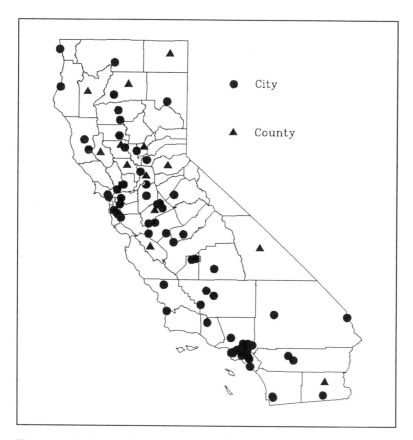

Figure 9. California Jurisdictions with No Growth Measures

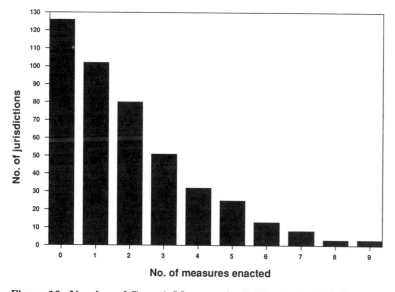

Figure 10. Number of Growth Measures in California Jurisdictions

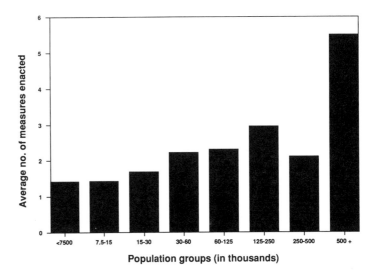

Figure 11. Relationship between Growth Measures and Population Size of Jurisdictions

These two jurisdictions have enacted the greatest variety of growth measures of all jurisdictions in California. Figure 11 also shows another exception: there is a "dip" in the average number of measures enacted among jurisdictions with populations of 250,000 to 500,000. Some examples are: Oakland—1; Sacramento—0; Anaheim—0; Santa Ana—1; Stockton—0; Bakersfield—0; Long Beach—1; and Glendale—2. Many of these cities are growing but have chosen not to enact growth controls. Future research is needed to understand why these medium-large cities tend to use less formal growth control.

Table 1 presents some summary statistics for the number of growth control and management measures enacted. The average number of measures is higher in jurisdictions that consider themselves metropolitan (2.1) than in those jurisdictions that consider themselves rural (1.7); however, this difference is *not* statistically significant. In addition, Table 1 shows that county jurisdictions have enacted or have pending slightly more measures on average in unincorporated areas (2.1) than have city jurisdictions (1.9); the difference is also not significant statistically.[34]

But there are significant differences between the average number of measures enacted in each of the four major metropolitan areas of California. While growth controls and growth management measures may have begun earlier in the San Francisco Bay Area, as earlier research suggests,[35] the San Diego region has the greatest concentration of growth measures of any region in California. With 62 measures en-

---

34. This trend for overall enacted and pending growth measures runs counter to the trends analyzed for ballot measures, where such measures have been recently found to be more successfully enacted in cities than in counties. See Madelyn Glickfeld, "Growth Control By Initiative and Referenda: An Overview and Update" (Conference Materials, Annual Land Use Law and Planning Conference, UCLA Extension, Public Policy Program, 27 January 1989), 16–17.

35. See Glickfeld, Graymer, and Morrison, "Trends in Local Growth Control Ballot Measures in California," UCLA *Journal of Environmental Law and Policy* (1987): 6:2.

acted and 5 measures pending among eighteen jurisdictions, the San Diego metropolitan area has 3.4 measures per jurisdiction, with 89 percent of responding jurisdictions reporting 1 or more measures enacted. The San Francisco Bay Area, with 222 measures enacted and 10 pending among 99 responding jurisdictions, is the second most concentrated region of growth control or growth management measures. The Sacramento metropolitan area, with 66 measures enacted and two pending among 34 responding jurisdictions, mirrors the state average number of measures at 1.9 per jurisdiction.[36] Although the Los Angeles region has 262 enacted measures and 23 pending measures, which make it the single highest locus of growth measures of metropolitan regions in the state, those measures are spread among 146 jurisdictions, 42 of which have no measures at all. This large number of jurisdictions without growth control measures dilutes the impact of the large number of measures in this region. The average number of measures per jurisdiction was calculated at 1.8, lower than the state average.

Figure 12 shows the average number of measures enacted within counties and their constituent cities and gives one of the most telling pictures of the distribution of local growth controls and management programs in California.[36] In general, the coastal counties (except the North Coast), the San Francisco Bay Area, and the Sierras in the Lake Tahoe region have the highest average number of growth control or management measures. The far northern part of the state, the North Coast, the North Central area, and Sacramento County have the lowest average number of measures. The southern California area (with the

In general, the coastal counties (except the North Coast), the San Francisco Bay Area, and the Sierras in the Lake Tahoe region have the highest average number of growth control or management measures.

36. However, 39 percent of responding jurisdictions in that region had *no* measures at all and the high average number of measures is skewed by the relatively small number of jurisdictions in the region (34) and the high number of measures enacted by South Lake Tahoe (8), Placer County (5), the cities of Lodi (6) and Manteca (6).

37. This analysis is done based on the data in Appendix D, which adds up the number of measures enacted by the county and all cities within the county reporting, and divides by the number of jurisdictions to obtain a countywide average.

Table 1. Indices of Growth Measures

Area	Average no. per jurisdiction	Percentage of jurisdictions with one or more
All jurisdictions (n=443)	1.93	71.6
Metropolitan areas (n=297)	2.05	75.1
Non-metropolitan areas (n=146)	1.66	64.4
Cities (n=386)	1.90	70.7
Counties (n=57)	2.11	77.2
Los Angeles metro area (n=146)	1.78	71.2
Sacramento metro area (n=34)	1.94	61.8
San Diego metro area (n=18)	3.44	88.9
San Francisco metro area (n=99)	2.24	82.8

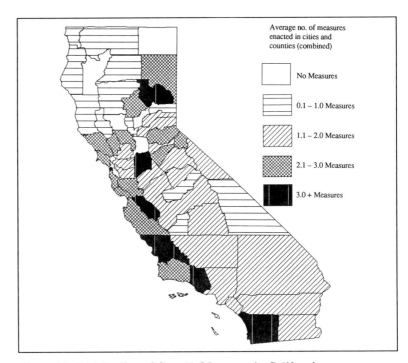

Figure 12. Distribution of Growth Measures in California

On average, communities with smaller populations are less likely to have growth measures than communities with larger populations.

exception of Ventura and San Diego counties) and the south central valley, southern Sierras, and eastern desert counties average in the middle, between 1.1 and 2.0 measures per jurisdiction.

Jurisdictions without Growth Measures

In our sample, 126 (or 28.4 percent) of the jurisdictions had not enacted any growth management or growth control measures. We examined the characteristics of these communities. As shown in Figures 8 and 9, jurisdictions without growth measures are slightly more likely to be located in rural and non-metropolitan areas than jurisdictions with measures; even though there is considerable overlap, the more rural parts of the state tend to have more jurisdictions without measures. Aside from this, the most striking difference is in population size. On average, communities with smaller populations are less likely to have growth measures than communities with larger populations; the average population size is 37,160 for jurisdictions without measures, compared to 71,653 for communities with measures. Aside from population size, there are only slight differences. Jurisdictions without measures have slightly *lower* per capita incomes (an average of $12,433 in 1987) than jurisdictions with measures (an average of $13,278 in 1987), and slightly lower proportions of high school graduates (70.5 percent compared to 72.8 percent) and substantially lower proportions of college graduates (16.9 percent compared to 19.3 percent). The ethnic distributions of these communities are very similar to those of communities with growth controls. The only meaningful difference is that jurisdictions without growth measures have slightly lower proportions of Asians (2.6 percent compared to 3.4 percent) and slightly higher proportions of non-Hispanic white persons (69.2 percent compared to 68.5 percent); all other ethnic comparisons are

within 0.5 percent of each other. In short, jurisdictions without measures are likely to be smaller and more rural than those with measures,
but, aside from population size, the differences between the two types
of communities are not major.

*Jurisdictions without
measures are likely to be
smaller and more rural than
those with measures.*

Types of Growth Measures Enacted

There is no one type of growth measure uniformly applied across
a majority of responding jurisdictions. In fact no one type of measure
is enacted or pending in any more than 29 percent of jurisdictions. As
shown in Tables 2 and 3, residential and commercial infrastructure requirements, residential downzoning, and commercial height limitations are each applied in about one-fourth of responding local jurisdictions. Greenbelt or urban limit line measures are enacted in 18 percent
of jurisdictions overall. Growth management elements, annual residential permit limitations, and rezoning of commercial land to lower
uses are enacted in 10 to 12 percent of jurisdictions.[38] All other measures are employed by small minorities of responding jurisdictions.

As shown in Figures 13, 14, 15, and 16, there are few significant
differences between the types of measures enacted or pending in
counties and those enacted or pending in cities. Measures that require
adequate infrastructure for residential and commercial development,
residential downzoning measures, and measures to reduce commercial
building height are predominant in both cities and counties. The only
type of measure for which a meaningful and significant difference occurs between cities and counties is urban limit lines or greenbelts, enacted by 40 percent of counties but only 15 percent of cities. There are

---

38. While growth management elements are only employed by a small minority of jurisdictions, and tend to be used by larger jurisdictions, many jurisdictions
that reported no particular types of measures enacted reported that they used the
general plan to manage growth.

Table 2. Percentage of Jurisdictions with Growth Measures

Type	All jurisdictions	Cities	Counties
Residential infrastructure requirements	29.3	29.2	29.8
Residential downzoning	27.3	27.5	26.3
Restricts permitted commercial/office building heights	25.6	26.3	21.1
Commercial/industrial infrastructure requirements	24.5	24.0	28.1
Urban limit line or greenbelt	17.9	14.5	40.4
Other, pending	12.2	12.2	12.3
Growth management element of the General Plan	11.5	11.1	14.0
Housing permit limitations	11.3	11.1	12.3
Rezone commercial/industrial land to a less intense use	10.3	10.5	8.8
Population growth caps	9.1	9.9	3.5
Other, enacted	7.7	8.3	3.5
Rezone residential land to a less intense use	6.1	4.9	14.0
Required voter approval for upzoning	4.3	4.4	3.5
Commercial square footage limitations	3.2	3.4	1.8
Industrial square footage limitations	3.1	3.3	1.9
Required council supermajority for upzoning	2.5	2.6	1.8

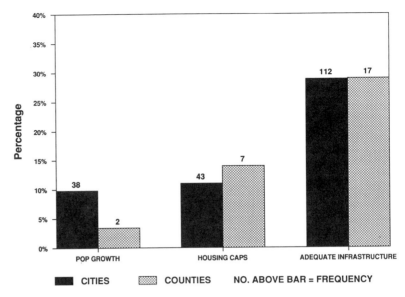

Figure 13. Percentage and Frequency of Jurisdictions with Residential Control Measures

smaller differences between cities and counties in their enactment of other types of measures, including population growth caps, a strategy employed by nearly 10 percent of cities and less than 4 percent of counties, and rezoning residential land to agriculture or open space, a strategy employed by only 5 percent of cities and 14 percent of counties.

Figure 17 shows the distribution of jurisdictions enacting urban limit lines or greenbelt programs. The large percentage of counties with such measures was unexpected. In fact, assuming that each of these urban limit lines was consistently implemented to restrict the extension of major infrastructure and urban density development, one could map each of these urban limit lines on a California map and have the rudimentary outlines of California's de facto state growth policy.

Table 3. Number of Jurisdictions with Growth Measures

Type	All jurisdictions	Cities	Counties
Residential infrastructure requirements	129	112	17
Residential downzoning	121	106	15
Restricts permitted commercial/office building heights	112	100	12
Commercial/industrial infrastructure requirements	108	92	16
Urban limit line or greenbelt	79	56	23
Other, pending	54	47	7
Growth management element of the General Plan	51	43	8
Housing permit limitations	50	43	7
Rezone commercial/industrial land to a less intense use	45	40	5
Population growth caps	40	38	2
Other, enacted	34	32	2
Rezone residential land to a less intense use	27	19	8
Required voter approval for upzoning	19	17	2
Commercial square footage limitations	14	13	1
Industrial square footage limitations	13	12	1
Required council supermajority for upzoning	11	10	1

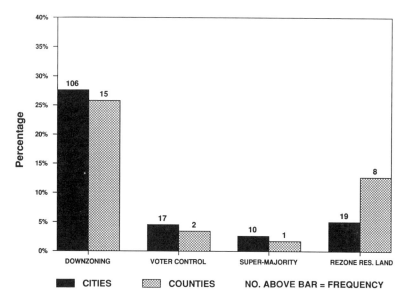

Figure 14. Percentage and Frequency of Jurisdictions with Residential Zoning Measures

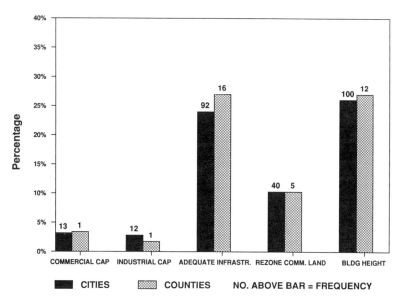

Figure 15. Percentage and Frequency of Jurisdictions with Commercial Measures

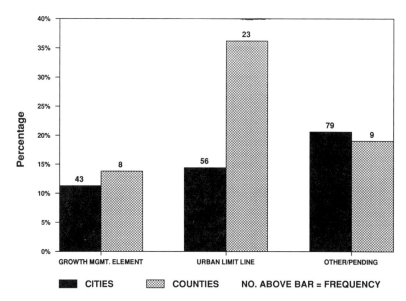

Figure 16. Percentage and Frequency of Jurisdictions with Planning and Other Measures

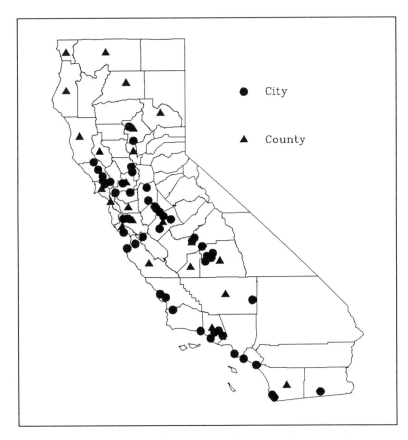

Figure 17. Jurisdictions with Urban Limit Lines or Greenbelts

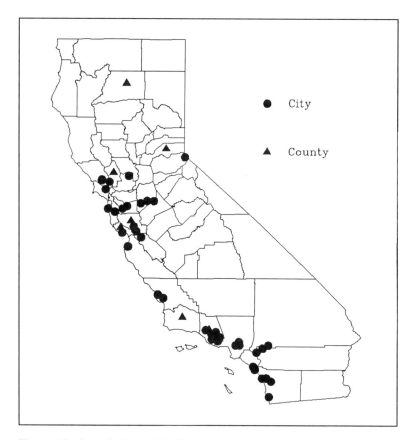

Figure 18. Jurisdictions with Housing Permit Limitations

While local population caps and residential permit controls are the most controversial types of measures enacted in California, they are employed by only a minority of jurisdictions. As seen in Tables 2 and 3, only thirty-eight cities and two counties have population growth limits. Only forty-three cities and seven counties have housing permit limits over a specified period of time. There is substantial overlap between these two measures; they tend to be enacted in the same jurisdictions. Figure 18 shows the geographic distribution of cities and counties with housing permit limitations. These jurisdictions tend to be smaller and distributed along the coast, in Riverside and San Bernardino counties, in San Joaquin County, and near Lake Tahoe. In other words, these jurisdictions are relatively few, tend to be small, and are scattered all over California. Our analysis indicated that they are probably too small and too spread out to have any effects on regional housing markets at this time. However, if more and larger jurisdictions enact this type of regulation, the potential for local population and housing caps to cause a subregional redistribution of housing is strong and is a subject for further research. Appendix D contains maps showing the geographic distribution of the twelve other types of measures identified in the survey.

Other Types of Measures Enacted and Pending

Thirty-four (or approximately 7 percent) of all responding jurisdictions have enacted measures other than the fourteen types identified in the survey. We have coded these into several categories (presented in the codebook in Appendix A). Many of these other measures reflect other means to accomplish the same ends as measures specified in the survey. There were, as of the first quarter of 1989, seventy-four measures pending in fifty-four jurisdictions (about 12 percent of the responding jurisdictions). Only nine of these jurisdictions were considering adopting a growth measure for the first time. Table 4 shows the frequency of these other enacted and pending measures identified by responding jurisdictions.

Many jurisdictions reported innovative and new approaches to growth controls, mainly in combining strategies. For instance, in the city of Antioch, the general plan sets up criteria for expansion into future urbanization areas. The growth management element of the general plan requires annual monitoring of service levels and a capital improvements program that maintains the desired levels of service. The city of Brentwood has an ordinance that ties residential development approvals directly to financing mechanisms to expand appropriate infrastructure. The city of Newport Beach has adopted a traffic phasing program and a set of commercial floor area ratios to link development standards to traffic. The city of Mountain View notes that its participation with Santa Clara County and surrounding cities to deal with greater-than-local problems has resulted in local policy changes to address these larger problems. In the Central Valley, Stanislaus County and the city of Turlock have developed an informal tax sharing arrangement to limit growth to inside the city limits rather than have the county open up outlying agricultural areas to development. Each year the city calculates the amount of sales tax gained through this agreement and makes a payment to the county out of its general fund to share some proportion of the sales tax. There is now a discussion between the county and other cities to implement similar agreements. In Contra Costa County, the city of Clayton reported that discussions between the county and its cities may lead to a countywide growth management program, accompanied by a sales tax transfer agreement.

Table 4. Number of Jurisdictions with Other Growth Measures

Type	Enacted	Pending
General plan, specific plan, zoning	3	24
Fees, taxes, adequate infrastructure requirements	10	13
Open space requirements, density restrictions	10	18
Control rate of growth	5	7
Control commercial growth	6	3
Other: voter control, temporary measures, study measures, jobs/housing balance, urban/rural boundary	6	9
Total	40	74
No. of jurisdictions	31	54

A similar comprehensive effort, undertaken by Marin County and its constituent cities, is evolving. An organized effort to raise the sales tax in the county to fund transportation improvements has been linked with several comprehensive objectives, including the development of eligibility requirements for local jurisdictions to receive transportation funds. These requirements include local participation in a regional planning process administered by a countywide planning agency implemented through a joint powers agreement. After formation, this agency will establish countywide standards for traffic, housing, water and sewer facilities, and environmental protection. It will also review local plans for conformance to those countywide standards. It will approve local annual growth limits established by traffic trip-allocation criteria. Local governments will be required to develop traffic level-of-service standards and a five-year capital improvements program to meet those standards. They will also be required to establish traffic mitigation fees and to consider non-roadway transportation projects. Jurisdictions that do not comply with these eligibility requirements would not receive local transportation improvement funds. The ballot measure for the sales tax failed in the November 1990 election, but discussions continue toward consensus.

Method of Adoption of Different Types of Growth Measures

The survey asked respondents to identify whether particular types of measures were adopted through citizen initiative or through the normal local government ordinance adoption process.[39] The issue is important because it has been widely assumed that the growth control movement is primarily a rebellion of the voters through the ballot box. Of the 907 types of measures reported in the survey, the method of adoption was identified for 799 measures (or 88 percent of the reported measures). Contrary to our expectation, the significant majority of growth measures—684 (or 85.6 percent)—were adopted by local government actions rather than by citizen initiative. Only 13.4 percent of measures identified in the survey were adopted through initiative, with an additional 1 percent adopted both through citizen initiative and local government ordinance.

There are some significant differences between the types of measures adopted by local government and those adopted by initiative. For instance, while only 13.4 percent of all measures were enacted by initiative, of the fifteen enacted measures requiring voter approval to increase residential densities, thirteen (or 87 percent) were adopted by initiative. Nearly 39 percent of all population cap measures and 28 percent of all housing cap measures were adopted by initiative, as were 29 percent of measures requiring a supermajority vote to increase residential densities.

Since growth control or management programs tend to be controversial, the survey was designed with the assumption that all measures are adopted by local government through either initiative or formal ordinance processes. This turned out to be an incorrect assumption. Many respondents reported adopting growth measures through less

Contrary to our expectation, the significant majority of growth measures—684 (or 85.6 percent)—were adopted by local government actions rather than by citizen initiative.

---

39. This issue was not addressed for growth management elements of the general plan.

Surprisingly, there is no simple relationship between the number of growth measures enacted and the population growth rate in the enacting jurisdiction.

formal means, either through council resolution or through directly implementing general plan policy without ordinances. Of the 684 measures adopted by the local government processes, 64.2 percent were reported to be adopted by ordinance, while 21.4 percent were adopted by less formal means, either by general plan adoption or by resolution. It should be noted that measures adopted by less formal means probably are implemented in a more discretionary manner than measures adopted formally through ordinance, where specific legal tests must be made for variances. Further research should address differences in the effectiveness of these measures based on method of adoption.

In addition, there were some differences in the types of measures implemented by local government ordinance as opposed to less formal general plan adoption or resolution. Less than 10 percent of population caps, housing caps, industrial caps, commercial/industrial infrastructure requirements, or commercial building height limitations were adopted through general plan adoption or resolution. However, this less formal, more discretionary means of adoption is the method of adoption for nearly half (48 percent or thirty-five) of the urban limit lines adopted. Therefore, while urban limit lines are a significant component of local growth approaches in California, they are probably less uniformly implemented than some of the other measures.

Nevertheless, the data indicate that the political initiative process is only responsible for a small proportion of growth control and management measures in California. Compared to the amount of publicity that has been expressed over voter initiatives in various jurisdictions, the overall direct effect is quite small. It is possible, however, that these initiatives were important in sending political signals to city councils who responded by passing ordinances to divert voter frustration. Certainly, a number of well-publicized cases seemed to suggest this scenario.

Growth Measures, Local Population Growth, and Local Building Activity

Surprisingly, there is no simple relationship between the number of growth measures enacted and the population growth rate in the enacting jurisdiction. To examine the extent to which actual growth in the local jurisdictions contributes to the passage of growth measures, we correlated the total number of measures currently enacted by a jurisdiction with measures of population and construction activity (Table 5). As shown, the single variable with the highest correlation with the number of measures enacted is the 1988 population of the jurisdiction. As we noted before, jurisdictions with larger populations tend to enact more measures than smaller ones. The correlation is not particularly high, however, and, as noted, there are many exceptions.

Several variables that are highly correlated with population size also tend to correlate with the number of measures enacted: the total number of housing units existing, the number of new residential units constructed in 1988, the number of single-family units constructed in 1988, the number of multi-family units constructed in 1988, and the total value of permits taken out for residential construction, commercial construction and total construction in the jurisdiction in 1988.[40] However, the correlation of these variables with the number of measures enacted is an artifact of jurisdiction population size; when combined in a multiple regression equation with population size (not shown), they are not significant, while population size remains significant. While population size of a city is significantly related to the enactment of growth measures, other measures of jurisdiction size are not. There is not a relationship between the land area of a jurisdiction and the number of growth control measures enacted ($r=0.02$). There is a significant but not very strong relationship between population density and the number of growth measures enacted ($r=0.12$).

The correlation between the number of measures enacted by a jurisdiction and the population growth rate between 1979 and 1988 is 0.04. The correlation between the number of measures enacted by a jurisdiction and the rate of growth of housing units between 1979 and 1988 is 0.01. In short, there is no simple relationship between growth in jurisdictions and the number of growth measures enacted. This lack of association to population growth is also true for the enactment of individual growth measures.

The lack of an association between growth and growth measures in individual jurisdictions suggests that several mediating variables

---

40. Population data for 1988 and per capita income data for 1987 come from the California State Department of Finance. Housing data also come from the California State Department of Finance. Data on residential units are for 1988. Data for permit valuation of construction come from the California Construction Industry Research Board. Data on the elderly population and the ethnic distribution come from the U.S. Census for 1980.

Table 5. Correlation between Population and Construction Characteristics of Jurisdictions and Number of Growth Measures

No. of jurisdictions	Variable	Correlation with no. of measures enacted (r)[a]	p[b]
443	Population, 1988	0.24	***
443	No. of housing units, 1988	0.23	***
443	Single-family units, added, 1988	0.09	ns
443	Multi-family units added, 1988	0.17	***
443	Total residential units added, 1988	0.16	***
443	Permitted value of residential construction, 1988	0.18	***
443	Permitted value of commercial construction, 1988	0.18	***
443	Permitted value of all construction, 1988	0.21	***
416	Population growth rate, 1979–1988	0.04	ns
415	Residential growth rate, 1979–1988	0.01	ns
443	Area of jurisdiction, sq. mi.	0.02	ns
443	Population density of jurisdiction, 1988	0.12	*

Notes:
* $p < 0.05$.
*** $p < 0.001$.
ns   p not significant.
a   Pearson product-moment correlation.
b   Significance level.

Contrary to prevalent expectations, there is no single socio-economic profile for jurisdictions that enact growth measures.

are critical. Later, we will try to show that growth measures are a response to regional growth, encompassing a far wider area than the jurisdiction. Jurisdictions appear to be caught up in broad regional growth, the effects of which impinge on individual jurisdictions and neighborhoods.

Growth Measures and Education, Age, Ethnicity, and Income

What types of communities enact growth control and management measures? It has been generally assumed that these measures are enacted by predominantly white, predominantly middle-class communities. The term "NIMBY" (Not-In-My-Back-Yard) has been coined to express a type of political movement often associated with citizen desire for growth management and control. Is there any truth to the assertion?

Contrary to prevalent expectations, there is no single socio-economic profile for jurisdictions that enact growth measures. Table 6 shows the correlation between several selected socio-economic variables and the total number of measures enacted. The proportion of the jurisdiction's population age 25 and older that is college-educated is slightly correlated with the number of measures enacted, as is the proportion of the population that is Asian (for both $r=0.13$); while statistically significant, these are not particularly strong relationships. Other socio-economic variables that we looked at are *not* statistically significant: the proportion of the jurisdiction's population that is elderly (age 65 and older), the proportion of the population in various ethnic groups (with the exception of Asian), and per capita income for 1987.

To examine the interaction among these variables and how they might account for growth measure enactment, two regression models

Table 6. Correlation between Socio-economic Characteristics of Jurisdictions and Number of Growth Measures

No. of jurisdictions	Variable	Correlation with no. of measures enacted (r)[a]	p
435	Per capita income, 1987	0.06	ns
346	Percentage high school graduates, age 25+ 1980 population	0.12	*
346	Percentage college graduates, age 25+ 1980 population	0.13	*
426	Percentage age 65 and older, 1980 population	0.04	ns
428	Percentage white, 1980 population	0.00	ns
428	Percentage black, 1980 population	0.02	ns
428	Percentage Latino, 1980 population	−0.03	ns
428	Percentage Asian, 1980 population	0.13	**
428	Percentage American Indian, 1980 population	−0.11	*
428	Percentage other races, 1980 population	−0.01	ns

Notes:
* $p < 0.05$.
** $p < 0.01$.
ns   p not significant.
a   Pearson product-moment correlation.

were developed for predicting the number of growth measures enacted. In the first, variables that are widely assumed to be correlated with the growth control movement were taken:

- Population size;
- Jurisdictions in metropolitan areas;
- Growth rate of the population between 1979 and 1988;
- Proportion of the population that is white; and
- Per capita income for 1987.

Population size is a control variable since it has already been shown to be correlated with the number of growth measures enacted. This model fits popular assumptions about the growth control movement, namely that it is a predominantly white, predominantly higher-income movement aimed at slowing down rapid population growth. We call this the NIMBY model. Table 7 presents the regression results for this model. As seen, only population size is significant; none of the social variables is significantly related to growth measure enactment.

Table 7. The NIMBY Model: Effects of Expected Variables on Number of Growth Measures (n=398)
$R^2=0.067$

Variable	Coefficient	Standard error	t^a	p
Constant	1.482			
Population, 1988	2.438×10^{-6}	4.826×10^{-7}	5.052	***
In metropolitan area	-0.035	0.208	-0.170	ns
Population growth rate, 1979–88	4.683	3.959	1.183	ns
Percentage white, 1980 population	-0.073	0.489	-0.150	ns
Per capita income, 1987	1.97×10^{-5}	1.81×10^{-5}	1.087	ns

Inter-Correlation Matrix (n=398)

	No. of measures enacted	Population, 1988	In metropolitan area	Population growth rate, 1979–88	Percentage white, 1980 population	Per capita income, 1987
No. of measures enacted	1.00	0.25 ***	−0.01 ns	0.04 ns	−0.01 ns	0.05 ns
Population, 1988		1.00	−0.05 ns	−0.04 ns	−0.09 ns	0.00 ns
In metropolitan area			1.00	0.09 ns	−0.03 ns	0.02 ns
Population growth rate, 1979–88				1.00	−0.08 ns	−0.20 ***
Percentage white, 1980 population					1.00	0.49 ***
Per capita income, 1987						1.00

Notes:
*** p < 0.001.
ns p not significant.
a t-test of difference between means.

Neither ethnicity nor income level appears to be related to the enactment of growth measures. Only the level of education of the population seems to be important in triggering the enactment of measures.

In the second model, a more descriptive framework was tested. Since several of the socio-economic variables are significantly correlated (e.g. per capita income and proportion college-educated), the socio-economic variables listed in Table 6 were factor-analyzed to eliminate the effect of multi-collinearity. Four factors were extracted (analysis not shown) and four variables having high loadings on each factor were selected:

- Population size, 1988;
- Population growth rate, 1979–1988;
- Proportion of the population that was college-educated in 1980; and
- Proportion of the population that was Asian in 1980.

Table 8 presents the results of this regression model relating the number of growth measures enacted in each jurisdiction with these four variables.[41] The level of predictability of this model is not very high; the R^2 is only 0.095. Only two of the variables are statistically significant. The strongest relationship is between measure enactment and population size, where larger jurisdictions are likely to enact more measures than smaller jurisdictions. Also, jurisdictions that had a higher proportion of college-educated persons in 1980 tend to enact more measures. The other two variables are not significant. The Asian proportion of the population in 1980 is not significant when controlling for population size and proportion college-educated, in spite of having a significant zero-order correlation. The population growth rate between 1979 and 1988 is also not significant when controlling for the other variables.[42]

In other words, there are few socio-economic correlates of jurisdictions that pass many growth measures. Neither ethnicity nor income level appears to be related to the enactment of growth measures. Only the level of education of the population seems to be important in triggering the enactment of measures, possibly suggesting that there is a greater awareness about the impacts of growth on land use and the quality of life among more educated communities. It is clear that the communities passing many growth control measures are not wealthy.

---

41. All regression coefficients are tested with a two-tailed t-test. There are two reasons for this. First, a two-tailed test is more conservative than a one-tailed test. Second, while some hypotheses are intuitive and can be set up a priori (e.g., a positive association between proportion of the population who are college-educated and the number of growth measures enacted), other relationships are not intuitive (e.g., the relation between proportion of the population who are Asian and the number of growth measures enacted). We therefore chose the more conservative test.

42. Some people have expressed a desire to predict growth control at the jurisdiction level using characteristics of the jurisdiction itself. So far, we have been unable to develop such a model beyond that discussed above. As we will show shortly, the phenomenon appears to be probabilistic for a much larger geographical area. That is, we will try to show that certain social and economic conditions trigger the incidence of growth control enactment at a broad regional level, but the model is not specific as to which jurisdictions pass these measures. There is an analogy here with the life expectancy table. This life table can predict with a high degree of accuracy the number of persons who will die each year (subdivided into age, sex, race, or any other social variable), but it cannot indicate which individuals will die.

While the popular image of the growth control movement is a white, middle-class group of homeowners who are resisting changes in land use, our data, and other research, do not support this interpretation.[43]

43. Our findings are consistent with those of Knaap, who found in a study of voter support for Oregon's 1982 state land use referendum that broad distinctions of social class may not sufficiently explain support or lack of support for state level growth management programs and that considerations of self-interest play a significant role in such support. He found that voter support followed popular perceptions about how the program resolved the complex issues of home rule, urban growth, and management. See Gerrit J. Knaap, "Self-Interest and Voter Support for Oregon's Land Use Controls," *Journal of the American Planning Association,* 53, 1 (Winter 1987): 92–97. Similar results were found by Baldassare in a survey of Orange County residents. He found that demographic and political factors were weak predictors of support for slower growth. Mark Baldassare, "Suburban Support for No-Growth Policies: Implications for the Growth Revolt," *Journal of Urban Affairs,* 12, 2:197–206. Finally, these results are supported by Neiman in his early finding, "Among a list of initial measures of socioeconomic/demographic measures, residential restrictiveness seems unrelated to social status (e.g., education, income)...." See Max Neiman, "Growth Control Project: The Mosaic of Intentions Propelling Regulation of Residential Development," working paper, (University of California at Riverside, n.d.), 8.

Table 8. Effects of Key Socio-economic Characteristics on Number of Growth Measures (n=323) $R^2=0.095$

Variable	Coefficient	Standard error	t	p
Constant	1.208			
Population, 1988	2.349×10^{-6}	5.022×10^{-7}	4.677	***
Percentage college graduates, age 25+ 1980 population	0.018	8.689×10^{-3}	2.073	*
Percentage Asian, 1980 population	3.955	2.612	1.514	ns
Population growth rate, 1979–88	6.278	4.896	1.282	ns

Inter-Correlation Matrix (n=398)

	No. of measures enacted	Population, 1988	Percentage college graduates, age 25+ 1980 population	Percentage Asian, 1980 population	Population growth rate, 1979–88
No. of measures enacted	1.00	0.26 ***	0.12 *	0.14 *	0.03 ns
Population, 1988		1.00	0.03 ns	0.14 *	−0.04 ns
Percentage college graduates, age 25+ 1980 population			1.00	0.21 ***	−0.24 ***
Percentage Asian, 1980 population				1.00	−0.03 ns
Population growth rate, 1979–88					1.00

Notes:
* $p < 0.05$.
*** $p < 0.001$.
ns p not significant.

*There appear to be six
distinct combinations of
measures that we have
termed "growth control
patterns."*

Measures Enacted in Combination: Growth Control Patterns

Since no single measure has been adopted by more than 29 percent of all jurisdictions, we examined whether or not jurisdictions enacted similar *combinations* of measures. In other words, are jurisdictions that adopt one type of measure likely to adopt other particular types of measures or to avoid enactment of still other types? To examine this, we conducted a principal component factor analysis of the types of measures to see if there were certain groupings or patterns of enactment.[44]

Our analysis shows that there are clusters of types of measures enacted. Table 9 shows the correlations (called "loadings") between each measure and each of the six factors. A positive correlation means a measure tends to be enacted together with another measure in the same jurisdiction, while a negative correlation means that the enactment of one type of measure is associated with lack of enactment of another type of measure. For example, Factor 1 shows the correlation of each type of measure with the grouping (factor). Three types of measures have correlations greater than 0.40 or less than −0.40 (population limits, housing permit caps and urban limit lines). Since the correlations of these three are positive, we can say that jurisdictions that have enacted any one of these three are more likely to have adopted one of the others.

Table 10 summarizes and labels the grouping of measures into factors. There appear to be six distinct combinations of measures that we have termed "growth control patterns": population control, floor space control, infrastructure control, zoning control, political control, and general control. Within each of these patterns, jurisdictions that adopt one of the measures are likely to adopt others within the same pattern. They may be viewed as six approaches taken by California local governments to address growth issues. As stated above, the first factor, or growth control pattern, has strong associations between the enactment of population limitation measures and housing permit limitation measures and a weaker association for enacting an urban limit line or greenbelt. We have named this factor *Population Control*.[45]

44. Factor analysis is a technique that groups variables together based on their correlations with each other and on their similar pattern of correlation with the other variables. A principal component factor analysis was conducted on the fifteen growth measures using the *SYSTAT FACTOR* program (See Leland Wilkinson, *SYSTAT: The System of Statistics* (Evanston, IL: SYSTAT, Inc., 1988). Since all variables are binomial (i.e., the jurisdiction either enacted the measure or did not), correlations between measures indicate similar likelihood of enactment. All factors having eigenvalues greater than 1 were extracted and then rotated according to the Varimax criteria. For details, see H.H. Harman, *Modern Factor Analysis,* 3rd ed. (Chicago: University of Chicago Press, 1976). The rotated solution produced six factors.

45. The weaker loading on the urban limit line or greenbelt can be partially explained by geographic regional differences. The three strategies, population caps, housing caps, and urban limit lines do tend to be enacted together in coastal county jurisdictions. However, the majority of Central Valley jurisdictions enacting urban limit lines do not also enact population or housing caps. This difference can be attributed to the different goals sought in these two geographic regions, with the Central Valley jurisdictions focussed on preserving agricultural lands through the urban limit line, while coastal jurisdictions use urban limit lines as much for growth rate control as for agricultural preservation.

The second factor has a strong association with enactment of measures that place a ceiling on both commercial and industrial square footage, with weaker associations for the enactment of measures to rezone commercial land, place commercial building height limits, or impose housing permit caps. We have named this factor *Floor Space Control*. The third factor has strong associations for the enactment of measures that require adequate housing service levels and adequate commercial or industrial service levels. We have named it *Infrastructure Control*.

The fourth factor has strong associations for the enactment of measures that reduce residential density and rezone residential and commercial land to less intense uses, with a weak association for measures enacting commercial building height limits. We have named this

Table 9. Factor Structure of Growth Measures (n=408)

Measure	Factor 1: Population Control	Factor 2: Floor Space Control	Factor 3: Infrastructure Control	Factor 4: Zoning Control	Factor 5: Political Control	Factor 6: General Control
Growth management element of the General Plan (q8F)	0.214	−0.038	0.076	0.102	0.028	0.728
Population growth caps (q9)	0.854	0.075	0.040	−0.043	0.147	0.055
Housing permit limitations (q10)	0.846	0.210	0.018	0.059	0.095	0.072
Residential infrastructure requirements (q11)	0.154	−0.028	0.910	0.025	0.043	0.041
Residential downzoning (q12A)	0.154	0.054	0.065	0.633	0.240	−0.058
Required voter approval for upzoning (q12B)	0.049	−0.064	−0.060	0.165	0.738	−0.011
Required council supermajority for upzoning (q12C)	0.100	−0.089	0.162	−0.034	0.687	0.190
Rezone residential land to a less intense use (q12D)	0.077	−0.149	0.034	0.751	−0.168	0.150
Commercial square footage limitations (q17A)	0.079	0.891	0.058	0.069	−0.055	0.111
Industrial square footage limitations (q17B)	0.174	0.842	0.005	0.086	−0.099	0.026
Commercial/industrial infrastructure requirements (q18)	−0.026	0.090	0.909	0.111	0.026	0.091
Rezone commercial/ industrial land to a less intense use (q19)	−0.012	0.338	0.021	0.630	0.061	0.058
Restricts permitted commercial/office building heights (q20)	−0.164	0.295	0.281	0.348	0.024	−0.085
Urban limit line or greenbelt (q25)	0.419	−0.244	0.167	0.182	−0.337	0.257
Other, enacted (q26)	−0.044	0.164	0.020	−0.027	0.112	0.806

Notes:
( )   Survey question number; see Appendix A.
underline   Loading ≥ 0.40 or ≤ −0.40.

factor *Zoning Control*. The fifth factor has strong associations for measures requiring voter approval to increase residential densities and requiring a super-majority council vote to increase residential densities. There are weak associations for measures that reduce residential density and for *not* enacting urban limit line measures. We have named this factor *Political Control*. Finally, the sixth factor has strong associations for enacting a general plan growth management element and for having enacted or pending other measures. We have named this *General Control* because it is not specific.

To examine the relationship between these factors, scales were created that combined the strongest items from each factor (those with loadings of +/– 0.40).[46] Table 11 presents the correlation among the six factor scales. As can be seen, there are slight correlations among the scales. Jurisdictions that have population control measures tend to also have general control measures. Also, jurisdictions that have service control measures tend to have zoning control measures. But these relationships are weak. Therefore, the six factors appear to reflect relatively independent types of growth control strategies by jurisdictions.

---

46. The factor solution produces an 'orthogonal' matrix. That is, each factor is statistically independent and each variable contributes to the factor even if it is weak. We used scales to eliminate any statistical effects of these unimportant variables.

Table 10. Growth Control Patterns

Population control

    Housing permit limitations
    Population growth caps
    Urban limit line or greenbelt

Floor space control

    Industrial square footage limitations
    Commercial square footage limitations

Infrastructure control

    Residential infrastructure requirements
    Commercial/industrial infrastructure requirements

Zoning control

    Rezone residential land to a less intense use
    Restricts permitted commercial/office building heights
    Residential downzoning
    Rezone commercial/industrial land to a less intense use

Political control

    Required voter approval for upzoning
    Required council supermajority for upzoning

General control

    Growth management element of the General Plan

Geographic Differences in the Use of the Six Growth Control Patterns

There are differences in the use of these six growth control approaches throughout the state. Table 12 presents the mean scores of the scales constructed from the six factors. Overall, infrastructure and zoning control approaches are used by the largest number of jurisdictions, followed by population and general control approaches. Metropolitan jurisdictions have used zoning control measures more often than non-metropolitan jurisdictions. Among the metropolitan areas, San Diego jurisdictions have passed zoning control measures more than the San Francisco or Los Angeles metropolitan jurisdictions have, which in turn have used these more than the Sacramento jurisdictions. In terms of geographical regions, zoning control measures have been used most by North East jurisdictions, followed by Central Coast, San Francisco, and South Coast jurisdictions (see Figure 6).

The situation is somewhat reversed for infrastructure control measures. Non-metropolitan jurisdictions have used these more than metropolitan jurisdictions. Among metropolitan areas, the San Diego and Sacramento jurisdictions have used these more than the San Francisco and Los Angeles jurisdictions. Among geographical regions, the highest use has been among jurisdictions in the Central Coast, Central East, and Central Inland. Population control measures have been passed more by county jurisdictions than by cities. Among metropolitan regions, the San Diego and San Francisco jurisdictions have passed population control measures more than the Sacramento and Los Angeles jurisdictions. Among geographical regions, the Central Coast, Central Inland, and San Francisco Bay jurisdictions have used these measures most frequently.

General control approaches (which involve having a general plan growth management element or passing an "other" measure) have

Overall, infrastructure and zoning control approaches are used by the largest number of jurisdictions, followed by population and general control approaches.

Table 11. Intercorrelation of Growth Control Patterns (n=408)

	Population control	Floor space control	Infrastructure control	Zoning control	Political control	General control
Population control	1.00	0.13 **	0.17 ***	0.07 ns	0.12 *	0.26 ***
Floor space control		1.00	0.06 ns	0.19 ***	−0.04 ns	0.02 ns
Infrastructure control			1.00	0.21 ***	0.08 ns	0.14 **
Zoning control				1.00	0.09 *	0.10 ns
Political control					1.00	0.13 **
General control						1.00

Notes:
Correlations among scales derived from factor analysis; see Table 10.
* $p < 0.05$.
** $p < 0.01$.
*** $p < 0.001$.
ns   p not significant.

Table 12. Geographic Distribution of Growth Control Patterns

	Mean (Standard deviation)					
	Population control	Floor space control	Infrastructure control	Zoning control	Political control	General control
All jurisdictions	0.377	0.057	0.539	0.693	0.068	0.315
(n=421–436)	(0.729)	(0.319)	(0.826)	(0.906)	(0.285)	(0.574)
Cities	0.350	0.060	0.533	0.691	0.070	0.318
(n=369–384)	(0.729)	(0.324)	(0.818)	(0.892)	(0.284)	(0.572)
Counties	0.561	0.038	0.579	0.702	0.053	0.298
(n=52–57)	(0.708)	(0.277)	(0.885)	(0.999)	(0.294)	(0.597)
Metropolitan	0.391	0.071	0.502	0.771	0.084	0.373
(n=282–297)	(0.771)	(0.351)	(0.803)	(0.934)	(0.323)	(0.609)
Non-metropolitan	0.349	0.029	0.614	0.535	0.034	0.199
(n=139–143)	(0.639)	(0.239)	(0.868)	(0.827)	(0.182)	(0.479)
Metropolitan areas						
Los Angeles	0.257	0.043	0.486	0.754	0.055	0.349
(n=139–146)	(0.697)	(0.266)	(0.793)	(0.901)	(0.228)	(0.582)
Sacramento	0.441	0.121	0.588	0.545	0.000	0.333
(n=33–34)	(0.746)	(0.485)	(0.892)	(0.833)	(0.000)	(0.595)
San Diego	0.556	0.000	0.778	1.056	0.389	0.889
(n=12–18)	(0.856)	(0.000)	(0.878)	(1.162)	(0.698)	(0.832)
San Francisco	0.541	0.108	0.444	0.818	0.101	0.327
(n=93–99)	(0.839)	(0.429)	(0.772)	(0.962)	(0.364)	(0.570)
Regions						
Central Coast	0.654	0.077	0.808	0.880	0.115	0.538
(n=33–34)	(0.892)	(0.392)	(0.939)	(0.781)	(0.326)	(0.706)
Central East	0.000	0.000	0.842	0.632	0.000	0.158
(n=19)	(0.000)	(0.000)	(0.958)	(0.597)	(0.000)	(0.375)
Central Inland	0.500	0.000	0.698	0.442	0.045	0.205
(n=43–44)	(0.731)	(0.000)	(0.887)	(0.825)	(0.211)	(0.462)
North Central	0.125	0.000	0.313	0.344	0.000	0.063
(n=27–32)	(0.336)	(0.000)	(0.693)	(0.787)	(0.000)	(0.354)
North Coast	0.250	0.000	0.417	0.250	0.000	0.000
(n=11–12)	(0.527)	(0.000)	(0.793)	(0.452)	(0.000)	(0.000)
North East	0.444	0.000	0.556	1.000	0.000	0.000
(n=8–9)	(0.527)	(0.000)	(0.882)	(1.500)	(0.000)	(0.000)
Sacramento	(0.441)	0.121	0.588	0.545	0.000	0.333
(n=33–34)	(0.746)	(0.485)	(0.892)	(0.833)	(0.000)	(0.595)
San Francisco	0.541	0.108	0.444	0.818	0.101	0.327
(n=93–99)	(0.839)	(0.429)	(0.772)	(0.962)	(0.364)	(0.570)
South Coast	0.325	0.049	0.512	0.806	0.094	0.422
(n=122–128)	(0.778)	(0.283)	(0.815)	(0.934)	(0.342)	(0.659)
South Inland	0.175	0.053	0.538	0.675	0.075	0.350
(n=38–40)	(0.446)	(0.324)	(0.790)	(0.917)	(0.267)	(0.533)

Note:
Means and standard deviations of scales derived from factor analysis; see Table 10.

been used more by metropolitan jurisdictions than by non-metropolitan jurisdictions. In particular, San Diego metropolitan jurisdictions have used these measures the most. Among the other two types of measures, political control has been used most in the San Diego area, while floor space control has been used most in the Sacramento and San Francisco metropolitan areas. In other words, different patterns of growth control appear to have been enacted throughout the state. There are definite geographic preferences for certain approaches to growth management.[47]

The Role of Time of Enactment of Growth Measures

The time of enactment of measures appears to play a significant role in determining the volume of measures enacted. Figures 4 and 5 documented the very significant rise in the volume of growth measures enacted between 1967 and 1988 for the state as a whole. The rate of growth shows almost an exponential increase, with a slow increase in the number of measures until the early 1980s, followed by an extremely rapid increase that continued to accelerate without peaking to our last data point in 1988. Therefore, while local governments have been enacting growth control and management measures for a long time, most currently enacted local growth measures in California appear to be of recent vintage.

While local governments have been enacting growth control and management measures for a long time, most currently enacted local growth measures in California appear to be of recent vintage.

We recognize that, prior to this rapid evolution of growth measures in local jurisdictions, other kinds of control measures were being enacted at the federal and state levels. And we know that there are other local government actions that are aimed at growth management (such as the imposition of fees). However, the recency of most enactments appears to be real. For example, we correlated the number of local measures passed each year with the number of growth measures submitted as local ballot measures,[48] and the correlation was 0.96. Figure 4 also displays the timing of ballot measures on the same graph as the number of growth measures that have been enacted. In other words, the time distribution of growth control measures enacted overall appears to mirror exactly the local political interest in these measures, as expressed by the number of growth-related measures brought to local ballots. While it is possible

---

47. Our findings are consistent with those of Knaap ("Self-Interest and Voter Support"), whose research did uncover significant geographic differences in support of Oregon's 1982 statewide land use referendum with support greater in the urbanized Willamette Valley than in the more rural areas, which are more dependent on resource extraction industries. Rural residents tended to be more suspicious of a state land use program that preempted home rule; however, urban residents perceived greater benefits from a statewide growth management policy than did rural residents.

48. See Glickfeld, Graymer and Morrison, "Trends in Local Growth Control."

The time of enactment of measures appears to play a significant role in determining which of the six growth control patterns emerges.

that our time data have errors, we believe that they correspond fairly closely to the true distribution.[49]

The time of enactment of measures appears to play a significant role in determining which of the six growth control patterns emerges. For each type of growth measure reported, we calculated the median year of adoption. Table 13 shows the median year of adoption for each type.[50] There is a gradual change in the predominant growth control pattern over time. The population control pattern is the oldest pattern, with a median adoption date of 1981. The floor space pattern has a split pattern. Industrial square footage limits are older, at a median adoption date of 1983, and commercial square footage limits are newer, with a median adoption date of 1986. Housing and commercial

49. There are, however, two sources of potential error for this curve. First, as mentioned earlier, about 30 percent of the respondents who reported measures did not give us the date of enactment. If the distribution of these dates is different from the measured distribution, it is possible that the shape of the curve would be slightly modified. Thus, there has probably been a slight undercounting of the number of measures for which we have information on the year of enactment. We analyzed the population sizes and land areas of jurisdictions where a measure was passed but where the date of enactment was not given. These jurisdictions are typically much smaller in population size and somewhat smaller in land area. Since smaller jurisdictions have tended to enact fewer measures than larger jurisdictions, the amount of undercounting is most likely small. Whether this undercounting has contributed to bias over the year of enactment cannot be determined. Most likely it has not. Second, since we measured only the date of enactment for the ordinance currently in place, we do not have a complete catalogue of all measures. It is possible that jurisdictions passed growth measures earlier and then amended them. Thus, the rapid increase after 1980 would be less muted than if we had the complete documentation.

50. Respondents did not give the date for approximately 20 percent of the measures reported; also, no date was requested for adoption of a growth management element.

Table 13. Timing of Growth Measure Enactment

Growth control pattern	Type of measure	Median year adopted	n
Population	Housing permit limitations	1981	41
Population	Urban limit line or greenbelt	1981	58
Population	Population growth caps	1982	37
Infrastructure	Residential infrastructure requirements	1983	101
Floor space	Industrial square footage limitations	1983	10
Zoning	Rezone residential land to a less intense use	1984	24
Infrastructure	Commercial/industrial infrastructure requirements	1984	80
Zoning	Restricts permitted commercial/office building heights	1985	84
Zoning	Residential downzoning	1985	110
Political	Required voter approval for upzoning	1985	17
Political	Required council supermajority for upzoning	1986	6
Floor space	Commercial square footage limitations	1986	11
Zoning	Rezone commercial/industrial land to a less intense use	1986	37
General	Other, enacted	1986	23

Note:
Date of adoption for growth management element in Master Plans was not requested.

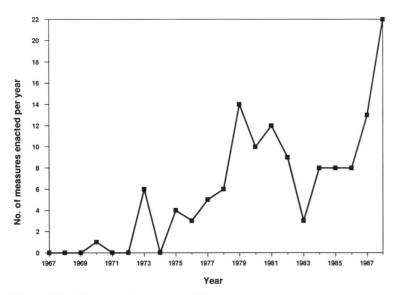

Figure 19. Change in Enactment of Population Control Measures, 1967–1988

infrastructure requirements follow, with a median adoption date of 1983 for residential and 1984 for commercial. Commercial building height limits, rezoning to lower uses, and residential downzoning are all part of the zoning control pattern, and the median adoption date goes from 1984 to 1986.[51] The most recent growth control pattern is that of political control, voter or super-majority approval for upzoning, with a median date of adoption of 1985–86, and "other" measures in 1986, which have a median adoption date of 1986.

We also plotted the trends for the six scales constructed from the factor analysis of the enacted growth measures. Figures 19 through 24 show the trends. All factor scales have shown a rapid increase in the last few years, but there are some subtle differences. As seen, population control measures started to appear in sizeable numbers in the mid-1970s, fell off slightly during the recession of 1981–82, then increased again. The infrastructure control pattern started to increase in the late 1970s and continued to increase throughout the 1980s. Zoning control measures are more a product of the 1980s, first appearing in sizeable numbers in 1980. Political control measures, while never very frequent, have been most intensely enacted since the early 1980s. Finally, floor space control measures and general measures have been more common starting in the late 1980s.

This evolving pattern of growth control approaches may reflect the changing nature of growth problems as they are perceived by local governments or pushed to the forefront by local ballot measures. For instance, the later predominance of controls on commercial development may be connected to the rapid emergence of suburban commercial development. The sequencing of different types of measures may reflect an instructional pattern as information is transferred from one jurisdiction to another. In other words, there may be "lead cities" involved in the timing pattern of growth control approaches. The lead

---

51. These results are slightly skewed by the fact that the survey only asks for height limit reductions in the last five years.

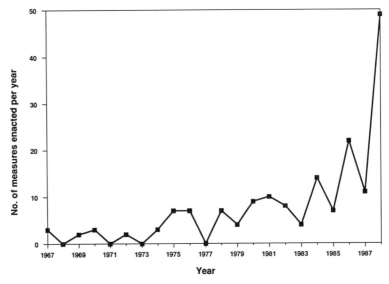

**Figure 20. Change in Enactment of Infrastructure Control Measures,
1967–1988**

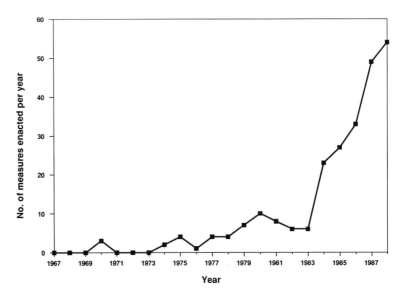

**Figure 21. Change in Enactment of Zoning Control Measures,
1967–1988**

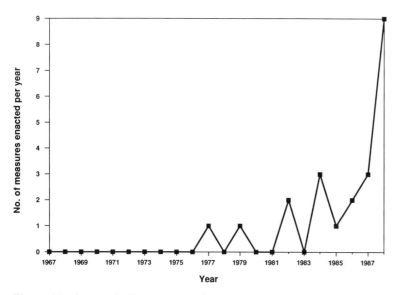

Figure 22. Change in Enactment of Political Control Measures, 1967–1988

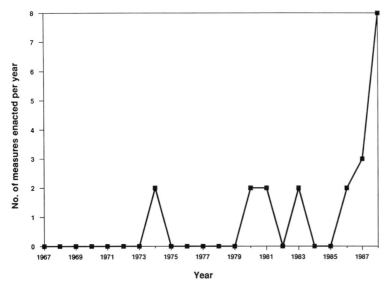

Figure 23. Change in Enactment of Floor Space Control Measures, 1967–1988

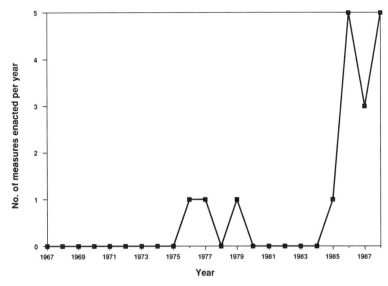

Figure 24. Change in Enactment of General Control Measures, 1967–1988

When we conducted a factor analysis to understand the reasons administrators give to explain the enactment of measures in their jurisdictions, we found that their responses tended to group into three categories of reasons: rural land preservation, urban population growth containment, and urban infrastructure protection.

cities may create an approach that is then disseminated to other jurisdictions over time. As the growth concerns in new jurisdictions increase, they adopt the same approaches the lead city did earlier. Our research cannot confirm that such a phenomenon exists, but it does indicate that further research on the topic is merited.

Reasons behind Growth Control Measures as Seen by Responding Jurisdictions

Why are growth measures enacted with increasing frequency? For those jurisdictions that had either residential or commercial measures, we asked the administrators who filled out the questionnaire to identify the main purposes behind each enacted measure; these were separated into reasons for residential measures and reasons for commercial/industrial measures. The reasons given are indicative of the larger-than-local types of regional phenomena described in the introduction (Tables 14 and 15). Generally, the most prominent reasons are related to urban growth and, for both residential measures and commercial measures, the order of importance is approximately the same. Preserving the "quality of life" and reducing traffic are the two reasons most selected, followed by sewer capacity and water quantity limitations. Reducing urban sprawl, protecting sensitive environmental areas, preserving open space, and preserving agricultural land are less frequently cited reasons. Finally, for residential measures only, respondents were allowed to indicate whether the quantity of high-density or low-income housing developments was the reason behind enacted measures; these were less frequently chosen than the others.

When we conducted a factor analysis to understand the reasons administrators give to explain the enactment of measures in their jurisdictions, we found that their responses tended to group into three categories of reasons: rural land preservation, urban population growth containment, and urban infrastructure protection (Table 16).[52] The first factor includes limiting urban sprawl, preserving open space, preserving agricultural land, and protecting sensitive environmental areas. We call it *Rural Land Preservation*. The second factor is a grouping of rapid population/housing growth, reduction in traffic congestion, quality of life preservation, the perception of the quantity of high-density housing developments, and the perception of the quantity of low-income housing developments. We call it *Urban Population Growth Containment*. The third factor includes sewer capacity and water quantity limitations, and the protection of air and water quality. We call it *Urban Infrastructure Protection*. The factor analysis of the reasons behind commercial measures produced an almost identical structure (not shown).

---

52. We conducted a principal component factor analysis (with Varimax rotation, using the same methodology described earlier) of the responses of these administrators and their perceived reasons for enacting the residential measures.

Table 14. Reasons for Residential Measures

Reason	Frequency cited by administrators
Quality of life preservation	98
Reduction in traffic congestion	93
Sewer capacity limitations	82
Water quantity limitations	63
Preservation of sensitive environmental areas	55
Open space/ridge line preservation	51
Rapid population/housing growth	46
Limitation of urban sprawl	46
Agricultural land preservation	38
Air quality	38
Water quality	37
Quantity of high-density housing developments	35
Quantity of low-income housing developments	14
Other	58

Table 15. Reasons for Commercial Measures

Reason	Frequency cited by administrators
Reduction in traffic congestion	70
Quality of life preservation	65
Sewer capacity limitations	50
Water quantity limitations	40
Air quality	26
Water quality	22
Preservation of sensitive environmental areas	20
Open space preservation	17
Limitation of urban sprawl	17
Agricultural land preservation	10
Other	48

The types of justifications administrators gave for the measures tend to differ in their aims, depending upon whether the jurisdiction is located in a metropolitan or a rural setting.

We have compared these factors with various demographic and economic indicators. It appears that the urban population growth factor is more associated with metropolitan areas, while the rural land factor is more associated with county jurisdictions and with large, exurban jurisdictions. There were also correlations with the measure typology developed earlier. Administrators from jurisdictions enacting zoning controls tended to justify these measures by rating the urban control factor, where administrators from jurisdictions enacting service controls tended to rate the urban infrastructure factor. Those jurisdictions with population control measures were rated higher on the rural land preservation factor. In other words, the types of justifications administrators gave for the measures tend to differ in their aims, depending upon whether the jurisdiction is located in a metropolitan or a rural setting.

There are three cautions that should be made in interpreting these results. First, these are perceptions of administrators. Their grouping of reasons appears to be more coherent and logical than the grouping of measures actually enacted. The factor analysis of measures extracted six distinct patterns (see Table 9), compared to three patterns of reasons. It is probable that administrators impose more cognitive coherence on the diversity of political reactions than really exists. Second, these reasons were presented only to administrators from jurisdictions that had passed growth control or management measures. Since those jurisdictions that did not enact such measures were not asked this question, conclusions about the generality of these perceptions are limited. Third, the perceived reasons are asked in general terms, rather than being tied to specific measures that have been enacted in a responding jurisdiction.[53] Consequently, we are not sure how well the reasons for enactment match the actual measures.

53. See Appendix A, questions 13 and 21.

Table 16. Factor Structure of Reasons for Residential Measures (n=443)

Reason	Factor I: Rural Land Preservation	Factor II: Urban Population Growth Containment	Factor III: Urban Infrastructure Protection
Quality of life preservation	0.332	0.636	0.286
Reduction in traffic congestion	0.150	0.616	0.442
Sewer capacity limitations	0.156	0.249	0.832
Water quantity limitations	0.114	0.071	0.817
Preservation of sensitive environmental areas	0.690	0.163	0.361
Open space/ridge line preservation	0.725	0.282	0.147
Rapid population/housing growth	0.149	0.690	0.260
Limitation of urban sprawl	0.773	0.206	0.180
Agricultural land preservation	0.837	−0.009	0.172
Air quality	0.355	0.240	0.616
Water quality	0.396	0.127	0.663
Quantity of high-density housing developments	−0.043	0.855	−0.074
Quantity of low-income housing developments	0.262	0.418	0.105

Note:
Underline   Loading ≥ 0.40 or ≤ −0.40.

Growth Measures and Low-Income Housing

Particular concern has been expressed about the effects of growth management measures on low-income housing. These concerns, expressed particularly by low-income or minority communities and the development community, have emphasized the potential negative effects of growth control on the construction of low-income units, especially in those areas experiencing rapid in-migration from abroad and from elsewhere in the country. To explore this, we asked each jurisdiction about its low-income housing policies.

Contrary to our expectations, we found some evidence that jurisdictions with growth control or management measures seek to plan affirmatively for both growth and housing needs. This conclusion is based on several relationships found in the survey. First, jurisdictions with current housing elements in their general plans are more likely to have growth management elements than those that have obsolete housing elements (r=0.13). Second, there appears to be a relationship between growth measures and various housing incentives enacted to stimulate low- or moderate-income housing (Table 17). Jurisdictions with five or more growth measures have significantly more active housing incentive programs than jurisdictions that have one to four measures, and jurisdictions with one to four measures have more active incentive programs than jurisdictions with no measures.

Part of this positive relationship between affordable housing incentives and local growth measure enactment is accounted for by population size. Larger jurisdictions have more measures, on average, than smaller jurisdictions. But even when we control for population size, there are significant associations between the number of measures and the enacting of incentives for affordable housing, such as density bonuses for low-income housing, special permit streamlining for affordable housing, and redevelopment subsidies for affordable housing. A multiple regression relating the number of measures enacted by a jurisdiction with the 1988 population of the jurisdiction, the passing of density bonuses, permit streamlining and redevelopment incentives for low-income housing yielded a model with a significant but weak R^2 of 0.14 (Table 18).

Contrary to our expectations, we found some evidence that jurisdictions with growth control or management measures seek to plan affirmatively for both growth and housing needs.

Table 17. Percentage of Jurisdictions with Housing Incentives by Number of Growth Control Measures

Incentive	Percentage of jurisdictions with:		
	0 measures (n=126)	1–4 measures (n=265)	5–9 measures (n=52)
Grant density bonuses	31.7	44.2	61.5
Issue revenue bonds	3.2	5.3	9.6
Streamline permit procedures	0.8	3.0	15.4
Obtain housing grants	1.6	2.6	3.8
Waive permits	1.6	4.5	7.7
Offer other financial subsidies	7.1	8.7	17.3
Offer redevelopment resources	2.4	4.2	9.6
Other	7.1	9.1	25.0

On the other hand, while jurisdictions that have growth measures tend to take separate actions to encourage affordable housing, jurisdictions that restrain growth most strenuously, through population limits and residential permit caps, do not generally exempt affordable housing from those caps. Only fourteen of thirty-nine jurisdictions having population growth caps exempt low-income housing from such caps; only twenty of forty-nine jurisdictions having residential permit caps report exempting low-income housing from such caps.[54] This may suggest that some communities are unwilling to address the direct effects of growth control measures on housing affordability.

We also correlated the number of measures passed by a jurisdiction with three indices of low-income housing need and production, as defined by a recent study on low-income housing in California jurisdictions:[55]

---

54. Some of these jurisdictions may give priority to low-income housing without outright exempting affordable projects from the caps.

55. California Coalition for Rural Housing, *Local Progress in Meeting the Low Income Housing Challenge: A Survey of California Communities' Low Income Housing Production* (Sacramento, 1989).

Table 18. Effects of Housing Incentives on Number of Growth Measures (n=359)
$R^2 = 0.14$

Variable	Coefficient	Standard error	t	p
Constant	1.4307	—	—	—
Population, 1988	0.0000019	0.00000048	3.91	**
Grant density bonuses	0.6964	0.1842	3.78	***
Streamline permit procedures	1.8742	0.4619	4.05	***
Offer redevelopment funding	1.0037	0.4675	2.15	*

Inter-Correlation Matrix (n=359)

	Number of measures enacted	Population, 1988	Grant density bonuses	Streamline permit procedures	Offer redevelopment funding
Number of measures enacted	1.00	0.24 ***	0.23 ***	0.21 ***	0.11 *
Population, 1988		1.00	0.16 ***	0.04 ns	0.19 ***
Grant density bonuses			1.00	0.16 ***	−0.05 ns
Streamline permit procedures				1.00	−0.04 ns
Offer redevelopment funding					1.00

Notes:
* $p < 0.05$.
** $p < 0.01$.
*** $p < 0.001$.
ns   p not signifcant.

1. Total number of low-income housing units needed by 1989, as defined by the "Regional Share Housing Needs" assigned by each regional Council of Government to each local jurisdiction;
2. Total number of low-income housing units actually produced by either the private or public sector at the end of 1989; and
3. Total low-income housing production as a percentage of total low-income housing need in each location jurisdiction.

Table 19 shows the relationship between categories of growth measures and averages of low-income housing need, low-income housing production, and low-income housing production as a percentage of low-income housing need. The relationships are not particularly strong and are mainly an artifact of jurisdiction population size. That is, Table 19 shows that the average number of low-income housing units needed and the average number of low-income housing units produced significantly increases between jurisdictions with no measures, to jurisdictions with one to four measures, to jurisdictions with five or more measures enacted. However, there is considerable variation among these categories. When low-income housing production is calculated as a percentage of low-income housing need, the reverse tendency is seen—the percentage declines for jurisdictions with more growth measures. That is, jurisdictions with no growth measures enacted have actually produced a higher percentage of their low-income housing need than jurisdictions with one to four measures enacted, and these, in turn, have produced a higher percentage of their

Table 19. Relationship between Low-Income Housing Production and Number of Growth Measures

	Average no. of units (Standard deviation) [n] Jurisdictions with:			F^a	p
	0 measures	1–4 measures	5–9 measures		
Housing needed	881.8 (2608.2) [119]	1163.5 (2307.0) [252]	3681.3 (6896.0) [50]	14.32	***
Housing produced	136.4 (298.1) [102]	243.9 (495.6) [215]	663.3 (2188.7) [42]	5.83	**
Percentage of needed housing produced	44.0% (71.4) [100]	39.0% (79.2) [213]	27.1% (54.5) [42]	0.76	ns

Notes:
**   p < 0.01.
***   p < 0.001.
ns   p not significant.
a   F-test of difference between means.

Jurisdictions with many growth control measures do not produce any fewer low-income housing units than those with no measures. The sad fact is that, in both cases, very few low-income housing units have been produced at all.

low-income housing need than jurisdictions with five or more enacted measures. This relationship, however, is not statistically significant.

These are averages across all jurisdictions and must be seen in relation to their variances (standard deviation), which are considerable. When these variables are correlated at the individual jurisdictional level with the number of growth measures enacted, there are only slight relationships. For example, the simple correlation between the number of measures enacted and the index of low-income housing need was 0.28, while the correlation between measures and the index of low-income housing production was 0.27. However, the correlation between measures and low-income production as a proportion of low-income housing need was −0.07. Since both the number of low-income housing units needed and the number of low-income housing units produced are highly correlated with population size (i.e., larger jurisdictions have a greater need for low-income housing as well as a greater production of low-income units), these relationships virtually disappear when controlling for population size.

Table 20 shows the results of a multiple regression model predicting the number of low-income housing units produced in a jurisdiction, with the population size of the jurisdiction and the number of growth control measures enacted. As seen, population size is positively and significantly related to low-income housing production. However, the number of growth control measures is not significantly related to low-income housing production. While the model produces a negative relationship, this effect cannot be distinguished from random variation.[56] Thus, jurisdictions with many growth control measures do not produce any fewer low-income housing units than those with no measures. The sad fact is that, in both cases, very few low-income housing units have been produced at all.[57]

In other words, it appears that jurisdictions with more growth control measures tend to enact other measures that are designed to encourage the development of low-income housing, but that they do so primarily because they are bigger and have more of a low-income housing need. In spite of this low-income housing need, these jurisdictions do not produce more low-income housing than non-growth control jurisdictions, even though they are generally bigger.

---

56. If a one-tailed t-test were used, the negative coefficient would be barely significant at the $p \leq 0.05$ level. We are using two-tailed t-tests, however, because they are more conservative and because any prior expectations would actually be in the opposite direction (i.e., we could expect a positive relationship between growth control measures and low-income housing production, see Tables 17 and 19).

57. The Coalition report states that only 16 percent of the state's low-income housing goals had been met through the end of 1989 (California Coalition for Rural Housing, *Local Progress in Housing Challenge*). In a study of California planning agencies, Dalton argues that the preoccupation of planning agencies with regulation involved in implementing the general plans has restricted the amount of involvement that agencies place on providing affordable housing. See Linda C. Dalton, "The Limits of Regulation: Evidence from Local Plan Implementation in California," *Journal of the American Planning Association* 55 (1989):151–168.

Enactment of Growth Measures and Statewide Construction Activity Over Time

What conditions precipitate the enactment of growth measures? As noted earlier in Tables 5 and 6, there is no significant correlation between actual housing or population growth in a particular jurisdiction and the number of growth control measures enacted in that jurisdiction. Thus, growth measures do not appear to be a response to local growth per se. On the other hand, it is possible that the measures are responses to larger, regional growth. To establish an explanatory framework, we decided first to examine the issue by looking at the behavior of all jurisdictions in the state to see whether a model could be constructed to identify precipitating conditions and, second, to apply this model to jurisdictions aggregated up to regional and subregional areas of the state.

At the state level, there are very strong relationships between the number of growth measures enacted annually by all local jurisdictions and the annual amount of statewide residential and non-residential permit valuation. Figure 25 shows trends in residential and non-residential building construction as measured by the valuation of the construction indicated on the permits (in 1989 dollars) over a twenty-two year period, from 1967 through 1988. As seen, residential construction has increased over time, but with several significant drops due to precipitating national or international conditions (the slight recession of the late 1960s, the energy crisis in 1973–1974; the rapid increase in inflation during the late 1970s followed by the recession of 1981–1982). However, non-residential construction (commercial, industrial and public sector) has been more consistent over the period, showing

Table 20. Effects of Number of Growth Measures on Low-Income Housing Production (n=359) $R^2=0.82$

Variable	Coefficient	Standard error	t	p
Intercept	43.844	—	—	—
Population size, 1988	0.00377	0.0000945	39.92	***
No. of measures enacted	–16.842	10.202	–1.65	ns

Inter-Correlation Matrix (n=359)

	Low-income housing units produced	Population, 1988	No. of measures enacted
Low-income housing units produced	1.00	0.91 ***	0.21 ***
Population, 1988		1.00	0.27 ***
No. of measures enacted			1.00

Note:
*** $p < 0.001$.

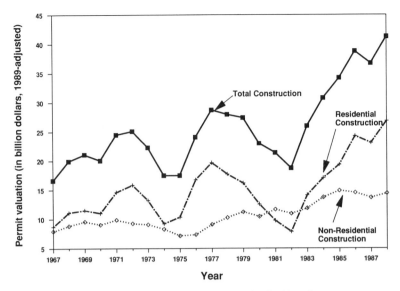

Figure 25. Permit Valuation of Construction in California, 1967–1988

While growth measures do not result from population growth within the individual jurisdictions, they can be seen as a reaction to increases in statewide non-residential building activity.

only slight reductions during these periods. Total construction (which is the sum of these two types) shows an increase over time, with decreases due primarily to the drop in residential construction. Eyeballing the trend line through these curves suggests that the rate of growth in construction activity has not declined at all over the twenty-two-year period, but may have even increased slightly during the 1980s.

We found that there is an extremely strong positive correlation between an increase or a decrease in non-residential building valuation (modeled as a non-linear quadratic function) and a concomitant increase in the number of measures enacted *three years after* the permits were taken out (R^2=0.90). Figure 26 graphs this relationship between non-residential building valuation and the number of measures passed (both on an annual basis). The time lag effect between a rise in building permit activity and an increase in enactment of measures may be explained by the fact that valuation is reported at the time building is authorized through a permit. It takes about two to three years after permit issuance to complete a commercial project. In addition, time is involved in the organization and processing of new regulations. Three years, therefore, represents almost an immediate reaction to increased building activity.

Thus, while growth measures do not result from population growth within the individual jurisdictions, they can be seen as a reaction to increases in statewide non-residential building activity. On the whole, when people sponsor local initiatives and local governments pass growth measures, they are responding to real growth in the form of building activity, particularly non-residential commercial and industrial building activity. However, it is not generally a response to real growth in the enacting jurisdiction, but growth in a larger area. The sudden upturn in growth control measures during the late 1980s indicates a heightened political sensitivity to this issue as well as a re-

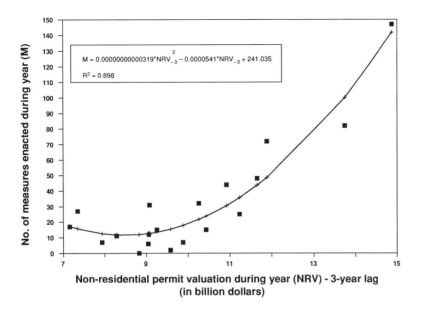

Figure 26. Effect of Non-residential Permit Valuation on Growth Measure Enactment, 1970–1988

sponse to a large increase in non-residential building three years prior; the quadratic function simply captures this accelerated growth rate. Our research does not show as strong a relationship between increases in residential permit activity, as measured by either the changes in the numbers of residential units built annually or the valuation of residential permits issued annually, and the later enactment of growth measures.

4

A MODEL OF GROWTH MEASURE ENACTMENT AND EFFECTS

Much of the traditional literature on cities assumes that local jurisdictions encourage growth in order to gain population, employment, and income. However, our data indicate that, at some critical point, the negative effects of growth start to outweigh the positive benefits, because of the rate of growth, the type of growth, the location of growth, or the inability to pace growth with adequate infrastructure.

In order to conceptualize the rather complex set of factors that influence the enactment of growth measures, we established a conceptual framework (Figure 27). This framework can be used to test both the factors motivating the enactment of measures and the effect of measures on growth, and it can be applied to view the aggregate activity of local governments at the statewide, regionwide, and countywide levels. The framework is made up of two models: (1) Enactment—a model describing the factors that precipitate an increase in the enactment of local growth measures; and (2) Effects—a model predicting the effects of measures on growth after enactment. We will discuss each of these in turn.

Structure of the Enactment Model

We hypothesize that growth measures represent alternative strategies for coping with population and building activity by local jurisdictions at that critical point where unregulated growth begins to be viewed as a cost rather than a benefit. In Stage 1—Enactment, growth control measures are enacted as a response to three conditions: population growth, non-residential construction, and political signals. Population growth increases demand for housing, water and sewer systems, public services, education, and so forth. Non-residential construction, on the other hand, represents job growth and increases in demands for subsidies from the community for public infrastructure. It may also concentrate the work force, thereby exacerbating traffic congestion. Finally, political signals are concerns conveyed to the community's political representatives about the problems perceived by the community. There are interrelationships among these variables. Population growth stimulates non-residential construction, which, in turn, may stimulate future population growth. Both variables also trigger political signals, which are primarily reactions to population and commercial growth. In our model, we do not consider these interrelationships, except conceptually, but treat these three variables as exogenous.

The model provides that all three factors precipitate enactment of measures. However, some or all three of these factors do not necessarily occur in the jurisdiction itself. For instance, population growth in one jurisdiction may precipitate political activity that results in the enactment of growth measures in another jurisdiction. Conversely, en-

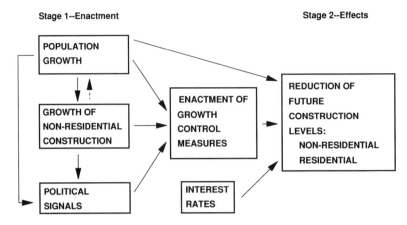

Figure 27. A Hypothetical Model of Growth Controls

actment of growth measures by the ballot in one jurisdiction may send political signals to another jurisdiction to do the same.

The model also reflects the cyclical nature of growth measure enactment. For instance, if the enacted measures fail to contain the negative effects of growth, the jurisdiction may attempt alternative strategies. Hence, the jurisdiction may shift from one measure to another as new kinds of growth problems become cogent or as prior measures fail to be effective.

We hypothesize, therefore, that three factors will significantly predict the number of local growth control and management measures enacted in the state:

1. There should be a *positive* relationship between statewide population growth and the enactment of local growth control measures;

2. There should be a *positive* relationship between statewide non-residential construction growth and the enactment of local growth control measures; and

3. There should be a *positive* relationship between political signals (either statewide or local) and the enactment of local growth control measures.

In the Stage 1—Enactment model, population growth is measured by population size modeled over time (rather than growth rate); it is the volume rather than the annual increase of people residing in a jurisdiction that places demands on the service system. Non-residential construction is measured by the annual valuation of construction as defined in the permits; this measure excludes the value of land and so is comparable across jurisdictions.[58] The model includes a quadratic

---

58. While this measure would be expected to represent a reasonable index of construction activity (and is used, for example, by the California Construction Industry Research Board), it is possible that the dollar value of construction masks some modifying conditions, such as the cost per square foot of construction and the additional cost associated with responding to existing growth measures. Still, it is probably the best measure available. The U.S. Construction Reports uses a slightly different measure—the value of construction put-in-place. These data were not available for California jurisdictions.

function and a three-year time lag to account for the time necessary for the local government to react to the increased construction levels.

A political signal is the most difficult of these concepts to measure. At least two different types of political signals seem to be important in activating growth control enactment. First, frequency of enactment of growth measures generally corresponds in time with changes in the frequency of ballot measures. Therefore, placement of land use initiatives and referenda on the ballot are a potential political signal to local government to enact its own measures. The governing bodies of many jurisdictions respond to citizen initiatives either by placing alternative measures on the ballot or by directly adopting measures. Second, in several instances, citizen initiatives have helped to propel growth control proponents into locally elected office, where they in turn encourage the enactment of measures. Political scientists and others should be able to expand on a larger variety of political signals that are associated with growth control enactment.[59] Recognizing the complexity, a simplified measure of political signals has been adopted for testing the Stage 1 model, namely the number of land use–related local ballot measures placed on the ballot in each year, with a three-year lag to account for a political response.

The Enactment Model at the Statewide Level: Evaluating Alternatives

Table 21 presents four alternative regression models testing the Stage 1 model:

1. With population size alone;
2. With non-residential construction alone (quadratic);
3. With both population size and non-residential construction (quadratic); and
4. With population size, non-residential construction (quadratic), and ballot measures.

As can be seen, population size is significant in the three models in which it is included. Similarly, non-residential construction is also significant in the three models in which it is specified. In model 3, both variables are significant, with non-residential construction being specified by a non-linear quadratic function. In the fourth model, ballot measures is not significant (but barely); it seems plausible that another political measure might improve the fit.

Thus, we conclude that, looking at the enactment of all local growth measures in the state over time, statewide population growth and changes in the total valuation of non-residential construction over time are the significant factors in motivating the enactment of growth control measures in California. Figure 28 shows the fit between the actual number of measures passed each year and the number predicted from population growth and permit value of non-residential construction.

---

59. For example, there may be competing political signals. Baldassare showed a distinction between the no-growth and the slow-growth advocates in Orange County; a majority of voters were in favor of policies that slowed growth, but opposed measures that were perceived as stopping growth. See Mark Baldassare, "Suburban Support for No-Growth Policies."

Autocorrelation was tested with the Durbin-Watson d.[60] From Table 21, only in the first model is there evidence of positive autocorrelation; this would be expected as the function is linear (population size) tested against a curvilinear dependent variable (number of growth measures enacted annually). In models 2 and 4, the test is inconclusive. Finally, the d for the selected model (model 3) falls above the upper limit. Therefore, there is no evidence of any apparent autocorrelation.

---

60. Samprit Chatterjee and Bertram Price, *Regression Analysis By Example* (New York: J. Wiley and Sons, 1977), 125–128, Appendix Table A.4a, 223–224. This tests the distribution of errors in a first-order autoregression, that is, whether errors at time t depend on errors at time t-1. The null hypothesis is that there is no relationship and that the difference in residual errors for the first-order autoregression is randomly distributed and uncorrelated. The test provides an upper and lower limit for the test. If the Durbin-Watson d is above the upper limit, then the null hypothesis is not rejected; the distribution of autoregressive errors does not significantly differ from that expected by chance. If the d is below the lower limit, then the null hypothesis is rejected; the positive correlation between the first-order autoregressive errors is greater than what would be expected on the basis of chance. If the d falls between the two limits, then the test is inconclusive.

Table 21. Stage 1—Enactment Models: Effects of Hypothesized Variables on Annual Number of Growth Measures in State, 1970–1988 (n=19)

Variable modelled	Regression coefficient (Standard error) [t]P			
	Model 1 (R^2=0.72)	Model 2 (R^2=0.90)	Model 3 (R^2=0.94)	Model 4[a] (R^2=0.95)
Intercept	−244.89	241.04	140.61	71.15
Population (no lag)	0.00001172 (0.00000176) [6.64]***	—	0.00000485 (0.00000152) [3.19]**	0.00000484 (0.00000190) [2.54]*
Permitted value of non-residential construction (3-year lag)	—	−0.00005400 (0.00001256) [−4.31]***	−0.00005212 (0.00001003) [−5.20]***	−0.00003617 (0.00001272) [2.54]*
Square of permitted value of non-residential construction (3-year lag)	—	3.188×10^{-12} (5.77×10^{-13}) [5.53]***	2.864×10^{-12} (4.71×10^{-13}) [6.09]***	1.933×10^{-12} (6.60×10^{-13}) [2.93]*
Ballot measures (3-year lag)	—	—	—	0.779768 (0.385168) [2.02]ns
Durbin-Watson d	0.85 **	1.52 inc.	2.20 ns	1.44 inc.

Notes:
* $p < 0.05$.
** $p < 0.01$.
*** $p < 0.001$.
ns p not significant.
a   1973–1988; n=16.
—   Variable not included in model.
inc. d is inconclusive.

In other words, it appears that the enactment of growth control and management measures is a response to at least two of the conditions specified in the framework—population growth and non-residential construction activity. In subsequent analyses, this model will be used. Why the accelerating trend (modeled as a quadratic function) occurs is not completely clear. Whether a critical population density or density of non-residential construction activity is reached or whether the political perceptions of this growth multiply cannot be determined from the data. It should be noted, though, that the trend is not linear but has accelerated rapidly.

It should also be noted that this model is plausible but not necessarily definitive. Since the number of data points (27) to test the model is limited and since most of the measures have been passed in the last few years, there is not sufficient variability over time to test the relationship clearly ; other series that increase monotonically over time could fit the data as well.[61] Therefore, we should be cautious and view this model as one of several alternative hypotheses.[62]

The Enactment Model in Metropolitan and Non-Metropolitan Areas

As was discussed in a previous section, there is no simple relationship between growth measures enacted at the local jurisdictional level and actual growth within that jurisdiction, as measured by either population, housing, or construction growth. This relationship was tested for only one point in time, however, and not as a series of measures over time. On the other hand, at the state level we see a very sizeable relationship between the number of growth measures enacted each year and growth in both population and non-residential construction over time. To reconcile this apparent contradiction, we hypothesize that the growth control measures are political responses to

It appears that the enactment of growth control and management measures is a response to at least two of the conditions specified in the framework— population growth and non-residential construction activity.

61. For example, the U.S. national construction data also fits the series well. The R^2 derived from including the value of non-residential construction *put in place* with California population size was 0.95, virtually the same as for California non-residential construction permit valuation. The time lag was also the same, which makes us question whether the U.S. data is measuring actual construction, valuation, or both. See U.S. Bureau of the Census, *Current Construction Reports,* various reports, 1967 through 1989.

62. Aside from these variables, we examined one other. For example, many commentators have suggested that the passage of Proposition 13 in 1978 put tremendous pressure on fiscal revenues for cities, thereby inducing them to encourage more growth. However, given the data, we were unable to show such a relationship. In one of our models predicting the number of growth control measures enacted in a year, a dummy variable was entered for Proposition 13 (before 1978 = '0'; 1978 and after = '1'); this variable was not significant when the other two variables were included in the model. We also ran separate regressions for the time period before Proposition 13 and the time period after; again, we were not able to show any meaningful difference in the regression coefficients (though the number of data points was very small for such an analysis). Therefore, while it is possible that Proposition 13 affected public officials' attitudes towards growth (though many officials we have talked to deny this), we cannot show any immediate effect. More sophisticated econometric models that examine year-to-year changes could conceivably show a significant effect, especially since there may have been a considerable time lag in Proposition 13's effects. Our model is not designed to test this.

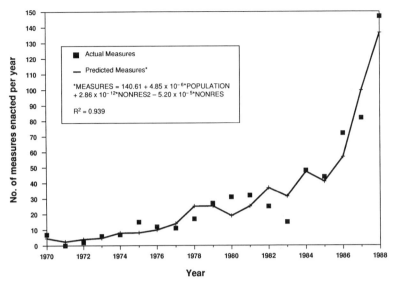

Figure 28. Comparison of Actual and Predicted Number of Growth Measures: From Population Growth and Non-residential Construction Valuation, 1970–1988

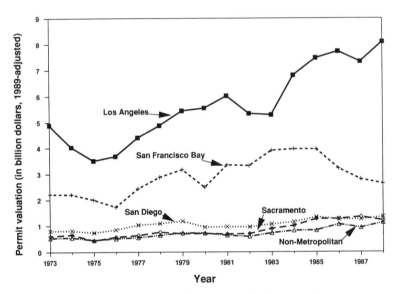

Figure 29. Permit Valuation of Non-residential Construction in Metropolitan Areas, 1973–1988

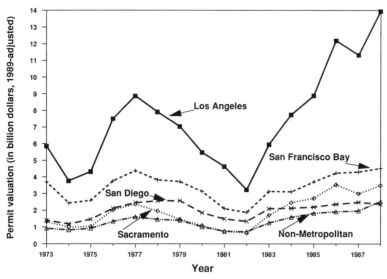

Figure 30. Permit Valuation of Residential Construction in Metropolitan Areas, 1973–1988

growth at the metropolitanwide level. Since there is no regional or metropolitan government in California, these measures are enacted at the only level available—local government.

To test this hypothesis, we analyzed the model for each of the four metropolitan regions and for selected individual counties within two metropolitan regions. In order to analyze the metropolitan regions, it was necessary to analyze construction trends within each of these areas. Figure 29 shows the trends in non-residential construction for the four major metropolitan areas in California plus the non-metropolitan areas. As seen, only in the San Francisco Bay Area has non-residential construction activity substantially declined, while in the five-county Los Angeles area it has continued to increase substantially. Within the San Francisco Bay Area, two counties account for much of this reduction: San Francisco and Santa Clara. In San Francisco, the reduction may be the result of several growth control measures. A downtown plan, passed in 1985, restricted office growth for three years, and Proposition M, in 1986, permanently reduced office space development. These measures have put into effect a program of fairly stringent commercial square footage limitations, adequate infrastructure requirements for commercial development, rezoning of commercial land to less intense uses, commercial building height reductions, and several impact fee linkage programs for housing and, most recently, for child care facilities.[63] Goetz also points out that the office space vacancy rate in San Francisco rose to 13.4 percent in 1986, which suggests that the market was saturated anyway. In Santa Clara County, some of the same types of commercial building restrictions have been enacted in San Jose, Palo Alto, and Cupertino, and to a lesser extent in Milpitas, Gilroy, and Sunnyvale. However, the reduction in commercial and industrial building in this county may be mainly due to a national slowdown in the electronics industry, which

63. Edward Goetz, "Office-Housing Linkage in San Francisco," *Journal of the American Planning Association* 55 (1989): 66–67.

is centered in Silicon Valley. Figure 30 shows the trends in residential construction for the same regions; all regions experienced an increase in residential construction after the 1981–1982 recession, especially the Los Angeles metropolitan area.

Table 22 presents the results of the Stage 1—Enactment model for four metropolitan regions and the remaining areas of the state (non-metropolitan). That is, we aggregated population, non-residential construction, and growth measure data for all jurisdictions within each of these regions. As can be seen, the fit of the model is reasonably good in several of the metropolitan regions. In San Diego and Los Angeles, the R^2 values, at 0.95 and 0.91 respectively, are about the same as the R^2 for the state model. In the San Francisco Bay Area, the fit is reasonable, though not as high, while in the Sacramento region and the non-metropolitan areas the fit is weak (for a time series correla-

Table 22. Stage 1—Enactment Models: Effects of Hypothesized Variables on Annual Number of Growth Measures in Metropolitan Regions, 1970–1988 (n=19)

Variable	Regression coefficient (Standard error) [t]p				
	San Diego (R^2=0.95)	Los Angeles (R^2=0.91)	San Francisco Bay Area (R^2=0.81)	Sacramento (R^2=0.72)	Non-metropolitan (R^2=0.54)
Intercept	7.50	79.68	10.01	30.29	1.69
Population (no lag)	0.00000173 (0.00000180) [0.96]	0.00000384 (0.00000116) [3.31]**	0.00000846 (0.00000393) [2.15]*	0.00000394 (0.00000303) [1.30]ns	0.000011344 (0.00000794) [1.43]ns
Permitted value of non-residential construction (3-year lag)	−0.00004074 (0.00000967) [−4.21]***	−0.00005008 (0.00000839) [−5.97]***	−0.00003888 (0.00001351) [−2.86]*	−0.00001524 (0.00000486) [−3.13]**	−0.00007171 (0.00008321) [−0.86]ns
Square of permitted value of non-residential construction (3-year lag)	3.877×10^{-12} (5.490×10^{-12}) [7.06]***	5.225×10^{-12} (8.003×10^{-13}) [6.53]***	7.477×10^{-12} (2.418×10^{-12}) [3.09]**	1.599×10^{-12} (4.663×10^{-13}) [3.45]**	4.242×10^{-11} (4.076×10^{-11}) [1.04]ns
Durbin-Watson d	1.54 inc.	1.98 ns	2.18 ns	2.22 ns	2.58 ns

Notes:
* $p < 0.05$.
** $p < 0.01$.
*** $p < 0.001$.
ns   p not significant.
inc.   d is inconclusive.

tion). The Durbin-Watson d is not significant in four of the five tests and inconclusive in the other; autocorrelation does not appear to be a problem in the analysis.

It is surprising that there is no regional coherence in enactment of local growth measures for jurisdictions outside the metropolitan area. We analyzed the Central Coast geographic region as the most likely non-metropolitan area in which measures could be a response to growth within the region itself. There was no significant relationship between population growth and non-residential construction valuation trends in the Central Coast and the enactment of measures in the area. Thus, enactment of local growth measures within non-metropolitan jurisdictions in California remains a response either to statewide growth or to growth in the metropolitan areas. That does not fly far from the comments heard in many rural areas about the desire to keep those communities from becoming "like Los Angeles."

However, the Stage 1—Enactment model works reasonably well at the multi-county, metropolitan level for three out of the four metropolitan areas. Population growth and increase in non-residential construction valuation account for increased enactment of growth measures in the San Diego, Los Angeles, and San Francisco Bay regions. Further, the strength of the relationship fits our expectations of the level of political sensitivity in growth control measures. San Diego has been the most active politically in generating growth control measures, especially in the last few years. In the five-county Los Angeles region, political involvement has been mixed; while there are many jurisdictions that have not responded to growth, there are many that have; for example, within the city of Los Angeles, which is the largest jurisdiction in the area. In the San Francisco Bay Area, growth control measures started earlier than in other metropolitan areas.

Population growth and increase in non-residential construction valuation account for increased enactment of growth measures in the San Diego, Los Angeles, and San Francisco Bay regions.

The Enactment Model at the County Level

The Stage I—Enactment model works at the state level; when statewide non-residential construction valuation and population rise, the enactment of growth measures significantly increases. Thus, growth measures are a real response to growth. The Stage I—Enactment model also works well for the San Diego, Los Angeles and San Francisco Bay metropolitan regions. In these metropolitan areas, growth measures are a response to actual population growth and non-residential construction activity.

To what extent do these relationships hold for counties? The Stage I—Enactment model was constructed for selected counties within the Los Angeles and San Francisco Bay metropolitan areas.[64] These are presented in Appendix E-1. An inspection of these tables shows that for the Stage 1 model, only in Los Angeles County, Orange County, and Riverside County is the enactment of growth measures meaningfully related to county-level population growth and non-residential building activity. These three counties are large and absorb a sizeable portion of the state's population growth; Los Angeles County, certainly, and, to a lesser extent, Orange and Riverside counties are regions in themselves.

---

64. The San Diego region was only aggregated at the San Diego County level. Thus, the regional and county models are the same.

Growth control measures appear to be local political responses to regional growth.

On the other hand, the model does not yield strong results for any of the individual counties in the Bay Area, nor for San Bernardino and Ventura counties in the Los Angeles region. In other words, we are seeing that, though the model works well at the metropolitanwide level, it does not work well at the county level, aside from the large Los Angeles, Orange, and Riverside counties. That is, growth control measures appear to be local political responses to regional growth.

In California, political jurisdictions can be quite small in area. The history of California has given local residents tremendous leverage to control their own land use, but little in the way of tools or mandates for resolving larger-than-local problems or interjurisdictional land use disputes. The state incorporation law allows citizens of unincorporated areas to declare themselves as incorporated cities as long as they can financially provide the same services presently generated in the proposed incorporation area. This tends to produce many geographically small cities that share borders with other cities. In Los Angeles county, for example, there are eighty-eight separate cities! Some of these are totally enclosed by the city of Los Angeles (e.g., Beverly Hills, Culver City, San Fernando). Thus, even though the growth control measures are being enacted at a local level, the phenomena they are addressing are regional.

In summary, at the state level, we find that the number of growth control measures enacted annually appears to be in response to population growth, to the growth of non-residential construction and, possibly, to political signals vis-a-vis growth control ballot measures, community activism, issue-dominated elections, and the like.

Structure of the Effects Model

Stage 2 of our model deals with the effects of growth control measures on construction activity. In Stage 2—Effects, the enactment of growth measures by all local jurisdictions or a regional group of local jurisdictions affects the volume of both non-residential and residential construction. That is, if the growth control or management measures are effective, then we could expect that either non-residential construction or residential construction would slow down a couple of years after enactment of a growth measure.

We expect that there are a variety of different ways in which this occurs. First, growth measures may reduce construction activity by actually limiting the amount of building that can occur. Many of the types of measures adopted would directly restrict construction volumes. For example, downzoning residential densities or rezoning residential land to agricultural or open space uses would definitely limit the volume of construction. Similarly, housing caps, population growth limits, and commercial or industrial floor space caps could slow development and reduce the overall volume of construction at any one time. Second, some measures seem to increase procedural difficulties for developers, thereby reducing the rate of growth. For example, requiring voter approval or a super-majority vote in a governing body for density increases tends both to discourage such requests and to lengthen the time it takes for a project to succeed. Third, some measures may add to the cost of development and, by so doing, may reduce demand. For example, adequate infrastructure requirements would add to the cost of development if improvements were feasible; or, if improvements were not feasible, the requirements would prevent new developments. Depending on market conditions, infrastructure improvement costs will result in either a lower demand for development or a higher cost to the purchasers.[65]

Some of the other measures that jurisdictions have passed may be more indirect in their effect. While not directly restricting the volume of construction, they may act to reduce the volumes of construction under certain circumstances. For example, urban limit lines will affect the location of development rather than the volume per se; however, if the amount of land within the limit lines is inadequate to meet market demands, then the volume of construction will also be reduced. In addition, downzoning of commercial land to residential uses will not by itself reduce construction volumes. But if land is redesignated to a use for which there is less demand, reduced construction volumes could result. Finally, since a growth management element of a general plan could include a spectrum of specific growth measures, it could, but not necessarily would, contribute to the reduction of construction activity.

Obviously, the impacts of a particular measure in a local jurisdiction are hard to gauge; even if effective, some measures will not necessarily restrict the amount of construction in the enacting jurisdiction, but may change the intensity of development, shift its geographical focus, or motivate the provision of adequate facilities. However, assuming that all measures enacted within a region were effectively implemented, and that no non-regulated jurisdictions were willing to absorb additional unmet market demand for growth in the region, we expect that the cumulative effects of all enacted measures would reduce the volume of construction overall.

Specification of the Effects Model

In our model, one possible effect of growth control measures on construction activity is examined, namely the total volume of activity. The actual variable used is the valuation of construction as indicated on the building permit; both non-residential and residential permit valuation are examined. There are clearly other effects variables that could be examined—distributional shifts from one type of construction to another, changes in the geographical locale of building activity, and changes in spatial density. We decided to focus on permitted building valuation because it is easily measured and available, and because it also would be expected to be the most sensitive indicator of shifts in building activity. Any changes in type of construction in a community would be expected to be shown in a reduction in overall building activity.

Specifying the independent variables is more complicated. In Figure 27, the Stage 2—Effects model, construction levels are determined by population growth, interest rates, and enactment of growth control measures. In turn, the enactment of growth control measures would be

---

65. See D. Amborski, J. Springer, R. Crow, and J. Mars, "Linking Office Development in Toronto to Affordable Housing: Policy Choices Based on Sound Evidence," and Andrejs Skaburskis, "Distribution of Burdens," papers presented at the 1990 Association of Collegiate Schools of Planning Conference, Austin, Texas, November 1990.

expected to have a delayed reaction, a function of the time necessary for the measures to take effect. In the model, the annual number of growth measures enacted is lagged by three years to simulate this effect. Obviously, this model is incompletely specified. Many other factors account for non-residential and residential construction other than these three variables, such as the availability of land and suitable infrastructure. Because growth control measures could account for only a partial effect, at best, on the volume and rate of construction, it is necessary to control for some of these other variables in order to determine the effects that growth measures play.

A simplified solution can be approximated by including two control variables along with the annual number of measures enacted: (1) population size, and (2) an index of interest rates. Population size is important because population growth is a direct stimulator of construction demand.[66] Interest rates are important because they reflect the continuing costs of financing construction, for both developers and buyers. In our model, we took the annual average prime lending rate because this rate drives most other construction interest rates.[67] In the model, population growth is not lagged, whereas the prime lending rate is lagged by one year.[68] The two variables in combination produce a very strong association with the permitted value of both non-residential and residential construction. By including the annual number of growth control measures enacted (lagged by three years), the effect of these measures on both statewide non-residential and residential construction can be estimated. If the growth control measures are effective, there should be a *negative* relationship between the annual number of measures and statewide construction activity, controlling for the other variables.[69]

We hypothesize that three factors will be associated with residential and non-residential construction activity:

1. There should be a *positive* relationship between population growth and the volume of both residential and non-residential construction in California;
2. There should be a *negative* relationship between changes in the prime lending rate and the volume of both residential and non-residential construction in California (i.e., when interest rates increase, construction activity decreases); and
3. There should be a *negative* relationship between the number of growth measures enacted and the volume of construction activity.

66. All population estimates came from the California State Department of Finance.

67. Prime Loan Rate to Large Businesses to Largest Borrowers. The data were taken from *Econ/Stats I: CD ROM* (Hopkins, Minn.: Hopkins Technology 1988), 518 in their reference. The data are in the form of monthly averages. We averaged these over a 12-month period to produce an approximate annual average.

68. We examined several other control variables for construction—the total value of U.S. construction put-in-place, a simple linear trend ('Year'), and the Gross State Product; various lag models were tried with each. None of these produced as good a result as population size and the prime lending rate; they gave the best overall fit with the least amount of apparent autocorrelation.

69. Because non-residential construction is measured three years prior to the number of measures in the Stage 1—Enactment model, but three years after in the Stage 2—Effects model, there is no need to control for simultaneity bias in sequencing the two models.

Statewide Results of the Effects Model

Table 23 presents the results for the Stage 2—Effects model. Separate regressions were constructed to analyze the effects of growth measures on non-residential and residential building activity respectively, as measured by reported permit valuation. As seen, the overall level of predictability is good for both non-residential construction and for residential construction. The Durbin-Watson d tests are inconclusive in both cases.[70] In both regressions, the effects

---

70. We examined possible autocorrelation from each of the independent variables. Population size does not appear to produce any autocorrelation for predicting non-residential construction, but there are some cyclical effects with residential construction. The prime lending rate shows some evidence of autocorrelation for both non-residential and residential construction; predicted construction levels were lower than expected prior to about 1980 and higher than expected thereafter. Growth measures do not appear to produce any autocorrelation for predicting non-residential construction, but there are some cyclical effects with residential construction, similar to the effects of population growth. These are individual effects, indicated by regressing each variable in turn against the two dependent variables. When combined in a multiple regression model, however, there does not appear to be any overall autocorrelation for non-residential construction, with only slight cyclical serial effects for residential construction prior to 1980. Overall, we do not believe that autocorrelation is a major problem with either of these models.

Table 23. Stage 2—Effects Models: Effects of Hypothesized Variables on Construction in State, 1973–1988

Variable	Permit value of construction, $1,000 (Standard error) $[t]^p$	
	Model 1: Non-residential (n=16) (R^2=0.87)	Model 2: Residential (n=16) (R^2=0.90)
Intercept	−$16,506,569	−$31,359,117
Population (no lag)	$1.174 (0.24) [4.88]***	$2.481 (0.45) [5.48]***
Average prime lending rate (1-year lag)	−$17,601 (69,726) [−0.25]ns	−$1,008,157 (131,220) [−7.68]***
Annual no. of measures enacted (3-year lag)	−$30,709 (39,167) [−0.78]ns	−$125,426 (73,711) [−1.70]ns
Durbin-Watson d	1.31 inc.	1.18 inc.

Notes:
* $p < 0.05$.
** $p < 0.01$.
*** $p < 0.001$.
ns   p not significant.
inc.   d is inconclusive.

It appears that individual growth measures do not significantly reduce the total value of construction.

of population growth are in the expected direction and are highly significant. That is, the value of both non-residential and residential construction increases as a direct result of population growth. Interpreting the models in Table 23 mechanically, each person added to California's population increases non-residential construction activity by $1,174 (in 1989 dollars) and residential construction activity by $2,481 (in 1989 dollars).

Similarly, the effect of the average prime lending rate is also in the expected direction in both models but is significant for only residential construction. Interpreting this mechanically, each percentage increase in the prime lending rate decreases residential construction by $1,008,157,000 a year. If the effect were significant by statistical standards, not random, each percentage increase in the prime lending rate would reduce non-residential construction by $17,601,000 a year. As was seen in Figure 25, residential construction activity in California has been much more cyclical over time than non-residential construction, suggesting its sensitivity to fluctuating interest rates and substantiating that non-residential construction is not significantly affected by interest rate.

Controlling for both these variables, however, the effect of the number of growth control measures enacted is in the expected direction but is not statistically significant in either model. That is, taking into account changes in population growth and changes in the prime interest rate, the number of growth control measures enacted annually cannot be shown to have a more than random effect on construction activity. In the case of non-residential construction activity, *each* growth control measure enacted three years prior would have reduced the value of statewide non-residential construction by $30.7 million. In the case of residential construction, *each* growth control measure enacted three years prior would have reduced the value of residential construction by $125.4 million. These would represent deviations from the expected trend line for construction activity if a statistically significant effect were found. They indicate an average reduction in construction activity due to each measure. The effects of additional growth control measures is stronger for residential construction than for non-residential construction; the coefficient is almost significant.

Even if the effect were statistically significant, it would still be very small compared to population size, interest rate, and overall level of prevailing construction. For example, in 1988 the total value of non-residential construction in California was $14.4 billion. The $30.7-million reduction in non-residential construction per growth measure represents 0.21 percent of all non-residential construction in that year. Similarly, the total value for residential construction in California during 1988 was $26.9 billion. The $125.4-million reduction for each growth measure represents only 0.47 percent of the total residential growth for that year. From a statistical viewpoint, such reductions are not significantly greater than what might be expected from normal year-to-year variations in construction activity. In other words, it appears that individual growth measures do not significantly reduce the total value of construction.

The model was also tested against the number of residential permits taken out for a given year. As with permitted building valuation, both population and the prime lending rate were significant, but the effect of additional growth measures was not. Even if growth measures were a significant causal factor in reducing construction activity, according to the model, each additional growth control measure enacted would have reduced permitted residential units by 2,475.[71] But compared to the 255,559 residential units that were permitted in 1988, such an amount accounts for about a 1 percent reduction. This reduction is higher than with the value of residential construction, but still not very large and not statistically attributable to the enactment of measures.

On the other hand, it is possible that the cumulative effects of growth control measures might have a significant effect on construction activity *if* they are truly additive, as specified in the model. In 1988, for example, there were 147 growth control measures enacted in the state. *If* each of these measures reduced non-residential construction by $30.7 million, then the total effect would equal a $4.5-billion reduction, or 31.3 percent of the total for that year. The corresponding figures for residential construction are a $18.4-billion reduction, which would be 68.5 percent of the total for that year. These latter calculations assume that the effects are additive, with each measure yielding a net loss of $30.7 million for non-residential construction and $125.4 million for residential construction.

To test this, we ran another Effects model, which substituted the cumulative number of measures enacted to date for the number of measures enacted annually. The R^2 figures were about the same ($R^2=0.86$ for non-residential construction and $R^2=0.92$ for residential construction), and the coefficients associated with cumulative measures were –$7.5 million and –$80.4 million for non-residential and residential construction valuation respectively.[72] Thus, the net effect of each *additional* measure shows even less effect on reducing construction activity than the *average* effect of each measure. It is probable that, even though 147 growth control measures were enacted

---

71. The results were as follows:

Dependent variable = Number of residential permits taken out
(in number of units)
$R^2 = 0.70$
Durbin-Watson d = 1.14/inconclusive

Variable	Coefficient	Standard error	t	p
Population (no lag)	0.028	0.010	2.90	$p < 0.05$
Average prime lending rate (1-year lag)	– 12,483	2,773	–4.50	$p < 0.001$
Annual no. of measures enacted (3-year lag)	– 2,475	1,558	–1.59	not significant

72. The cumulative effect on permitted residential units was only a reduction of 1,121 units per additional growth measure.

We suspect that the net effect of these growth control measures has not been very strong.

throughout the state in 1988, their combined effect is less than 147 times their average effect because additional measures appear to contribute marginally less. We must wait a few years to determine whether the total number of growth control measures enacted in the last couple of years will have any major effect on future construction activity.

In other words, we suspect that the net effect of these growth control measures has not been very strong. It is probable that some types of measures affect non-residential construction while others affect residential construction, but this result is difficult to test with our data. In the time period measured by the model, however, the effects of enacted measures have so far been negligible. For the second stage of the model, there is little to show that these measures have been effective to date in reducing construction activity. Partly this is because most of the measures have been passed in the last few years; thus, the time period is inadequate. But in part it may also be that many enacted measures are not able to stop population growth and non-residential construction; they may be only redistributing growth.

Table 24. Stage 2—Effects Model: Relationship between Hypothesized Variables and Construction in Metropolitan Regions of the State, 1973–1988

Variable	Permit value of construction, $1,000 (Standard error) $[t]^p$			
	San Diego		Los Angeles	
	Model 1[a] (R^2=0.86)	Model 2[b] (R^2=0.83)	Model 1[a] (R^2=0.87)	Model 2[b] (R^2=0.92)
Intercept	– $1,009,627	– $1,942,419	– $7,120,753	– $14,865,160
Population (no lag)	$1.078 (0.14) $[7.97]$***	$2.839 (0.49) $[5.80]$***	$1.120 (0.20) $[5.54]$***	$2.364 (0.32) $[7.35]$***
Average prime lending rate (1-year lag)	– $16,856 (8,060) $[-2.09]$*	– $149,727 (29,228) $[-5.12]$***	– $52,400 (40,873) $[-1.28]^{ns}$	– $515,323 (65,054) $[-7.92]$***
Annual no. of measures enacted (3-year lag)	– $65,708 (50,738) $[-1.30]^{ns}$	– $70,375 (183,989) $[-0.38]^{ns}$	$28,678 (50,769) $[-0.56]^{ns}$	– $68,759 (80,805) $[-0.85]^{ns}$
Durbin-Watson d	1.11 inc.	1.03 inc.	1.32 inc.	1.57 inc.

Notes:
a   Model 1: Non-residential construction (n=16).
b   Model 2: Residential construction (n=16).
* $p < 0.05$.
** $p < 0.01$.
*** $p < 0.001$.
ns   p not significant.
inc.   d is inconclusive.

The Effects Model in Metropolitan and Non-Metropolitan Areas

The Stage 2—Effects models are consistent with the state model at the metropolitan-region level (Table 24). The enactment of growth measures is *not* related to the valuation of non-residential construction in any single metropolitan area for both non-residential and residential construction valuation. Further, for the Los Angeles metropolitan area and the San Francisco Bay area, the direction of effect for growth control measures is opposite to what is expected for non-residential construction. That is, in these areas, growth control measures are positively correlated with *increases* in non-residential construction, controlling for other factors. In other words, whatever the reason for the positive coefficients for annual measures, they are clearly not reducing non-residential activity in these regions. Only in the San Diego and Sacramento regions and in the non-metropolitan areas are the measures associated with a slight, but not statistically significant, decline in non-residential building activity.

Table 24 (continued)

		Permit value of construction, $1,000 (Standard error) [t]^p			
San Francisco Bay		Sacramento		Non-metropolitan	
Model 1[a] (R^2=0.59)	Model 2[b] (R^2=0.78)	Model 1[a] (R^2=0.93)	Model 2[b] (R^2=0.90)	Model 1[a] (R^2=0.83)	Model 2[b] (R^2=0.49)
−$1,695,741	−$2,574,088	−$516,604	−$843,276	−$295,417	−$647,912
$0.661 (0.61) [1.09]ns	$1.451 (0.52) [2.78]*	$0.791 (0.07) [11.75]***	$1.758 (0.20) [8.63]***	$0.457 (0.08) [6.02]***	$0.564 (0.33) [1.71]
$72,779 (35,065) [2.08]ns	−$169,004 (30,229) [−5.59]***	−$14,798 (4,092) [−3.62]**	−$84,099 (12,377) [−6.80]***	−$15,375 (6,323) [−2.43]*	−$57,201 (27,408) [−2.09]
$47,108 (57,833) [0.81]ns	−$40,155 (49,900) [−0.80]ns	−$6,171 (8,014) [−0.77]	−$13,445 (24,237) [−0.55]	−$933 (3,610) [−0.26]	$9,827 (15,647) [0.63]
1.29 inc.	1.86 ns	2.33 ns	1.12 inc.	1.50 inc.	0.68 *

There is no evidence to suggest that enactment of growth control measures has reduced construction activity within the greater metropolitan areas of California.

For residential construction, the models also show that growth measures have *not* significantly reduced construction activity in any area. In four of the five regions, the direction of effect of growth control measures is negative as expected, but the effect is not statistically significant. In the non-metropolitan areas of the state, growth measures are in the opposite direction to that expected (that is, growth increases), but are similarly not significant in their effect.

In other words, as at the state level, there is no evidence to suggest that enactment of growth control measures has reduced construction activity within the greater metropolitan areas of California.

The Effects Model at the County Level

At the county level, growth control measures do not appear to have had a major overall effect in reducing construction activity.

Appendix E-2 presents the regression results for the Stage 2—Effects models for the same selected counties. Out of the thirty tests presented, in only two cases are growth measures significantly related to construction activity (with one other being almost significant). Only for Riverside and Contra Costa counties have the effects of growth measures significantly reduced non-residential construction activity.[73] These results are not indicative of a meaningful effect, even for these counties; two significant tests out of thirty represents a probability only slightly greater than our significance probability (i.e., 13.3 percent compared to 5 percent). In other words, at the county level, growth control measures do not appear to have had a major overall effect in reducing construction activity. This is not surprising given that these measures have not reduced construction activity at the state or metropolitan levels.

---

73. In Los Angeles County, the effects of growth measures are almost significant in terms of reducing residential construction activity.

5

DISCUSSION AND POLICY IMPLICATIONS

Conclusions

What can we conclude from this data? First, enactment of growth control measures in California has spread throughout the state's local jurisdictions in the last few years at an accelerating rate. Local growth measures are now on the books in virtually every region of the state. Most new measures are being enacted by jurisdictions that already have some measures. Second, larger jurisdictions are more likely to enact measures than smaller ones; further, the larger the jurisdiction, the more measures tend to be enacted. Third, while some types of measures are more utilized than others (zoning control, adequate service requirements), no one type of measure predominates.

Fourth, despite the high visibility of ballot measures, the vast majority of local growth measures are passed by local governments through normal public hearing processes. Fifth, there is no relationship between the rate of growth at the local level and the enactment of growth control measures. Sixth, there are only weak relationships with socio-economic variables. Jurisdictions that have passed more growth measures tend to have better-educated populations, but we did not find any support for the hypothesis that growth control measures are exclusively centered in white, middle-class communities.

Seventh, growth control measures tend to be adopted in six identifiable patterns, which vary by geographical location and time of enactment. The most common patterns are infrastructure and zoning control. Less frequently used are patterns of floor space control, population/housing control, and political control. Eighth, population control measures appeared earlier, from the mid-1970s, followed by infrastructure control measures. Zoning and political control measures are more a product of the early 1980s, while floor space and more general approaches have been more common in the late 1980s.

Ninth, according to the administrators who filled out the questionnaires, three types of reasons for the enactment of growth management and control measures seem to be common: a) urban population growth containment; b) urban infrastructure protection; and c) rural land preservation. Tenth, jurisdictions which have passed growth measures have also tended to enact low-income housing incentives. However, there is no evidence that these incentives produce a greater amount of low-income housing. Eleventh, growth measures appear to be a local response to regional growth rather than to growth in any particular city. When examined at the state level, there is a definite relationship between the enactment of growth measures and population growth and growth in non-residential construction. This relationship also holds at the metropolitan level but starts to break down at the county level. The relationship appears to be related to regional environmental, traffic and infrastructures concerns (at least as perceived by the administrators who filled out the questionnaires).

Different locales place emphasis on different reasons for enacting growth measures. Twelfth, and finally, up to the point that we conducted our survey, the growth measures do not appear to have had a major effect in reducing construction at either the state, metropolitan region, or county level. The measures may be effective at the local level—our data base is not fine enough to discriminate at the local level. But, cumulatively, the growth measures do not reduce the overall level of either non-residential or residential construction at the statewide, regional, and county levels (for the counties we have looked at). Whether this is due to the recency of these measures or to some basic defects in their design cannot be determined by our data.

Reasons for Ineffective Growth Management Measures

Most of the problems addressed by growth measures are regional in scope.

There are several reasons why these growth measures may not be effective overall in reducing construction activity at the metropolitan-wide level. First, *most of the problems addressed by growth measures are regional in scope.* The measures may be effective locally, but they cannot address the larger-than-local effects of regional problems. For example, traffic congestion is a regional phenomenon. If people live in one community and work in another, the scope of their travel frequently transcends local neighborhoods and small cities. Similarly, land prices are regional in scope; most economic indicators of real estate prices explicitly acknowledge the regional nature of real estate. Increasing land prices inevitably lead to higher-density residential building as well as higher-density commercial and office construction. Much of the anger seen in the recent wave of anti-growth protests seems to be aimed at large non-residential projects and, occasionally, at large residential projects as well. The urban sprawl, so feared at the exurban edges of metropolitan areas, is also a product of large regional population growth. The problem is larger-than-local.

Second, *there is still substantial demand for residential and non-residential construction due to increasing population growth (ignoring swings in the national construction cycle).* California's population has been growing at very rapid pace over the last ten years and at a consistently high pace for over one hundred years. As long as the population of the state keeps increasing, there will be pressure for additional housing and additional facilities to accommodate related jobs, services, and retail activities.

Third, *there is leakage in the system.* If one jurisdiction enacts strong growth measures (assuming they are effective), developers can usually move to adjacent communities within the same metropolitan area. The state's incorporation law, which has allowed small populations to incorporate as cities, has created a checkerboard pattern of cities within the metropolitan areas, hence a fragmented and inconsistent growth management policy. Without a state or regional growth management policy, it is relatively easy for developers to avoid the constraints of one community by redirecting growth to another community.

Fourth, *many of these measures may be political compromises,* watering down strict growth control clauses with numerous variances and exceptions. The real estate and construction industries work very hard at protecting their interests at both the local and state levels. The demands of existing constituents to control growth compete with demands for new jobs and housing. This often results in growth control measures where effectiveness has been hampered by compromise. For example, Dowall has argued that land use regulations help maintain the power of large developers in the San Francisco Bay area.[74] Many times, planning agencies are unable to carry out their intent to restrict development.

On the other hand, there may be little public support for strong growth controls. For example, Baldassare, in a survey of Orange County residents, showed that while slow-growth policies are consistently favored by wide margins, nevertheless a significant majority oppose measures that are perceived as no-growth.[75] He believes that the rapid erosion of support for a June 1988 Orange County Growth Management Program occurred because the anti-growth control forces were able to convince the voters that the initiative was not slow-growth, but no-growth.

Fifth, and finally, *many of these measures may be more symbolic than real in their effect.* The rapid increase of growth control and management measures over the last four or five years suggests that many of these measures were enacted under extreme political pressure without adequately creating a framework that could manage growth over a long period, and without a clear understanding of the enormous population pressures that confront California communities today.

Nationally there has been a great deal of debate about how effective growth control and growth management measures really are, whether they attain their goals, and if they have undesired side effects, both in the community of origin and in surrounding communities. Our data suggest that growth control measures in California have not been effective in reducing the overall level of building activity. However, since most of the growth control measures have been enacted in the last few years, the effects may not be seen for several more years. Naturally, we looked only at one consequence of growth control measures—construction activity—and we examined it from a global viewpoint. If other dimensions were examined, such as protection of particular environments, protection of open land, or maintenance of a balance between population growth and infrastructure, it is possible that a more positive conclusion might be found.

It is also important to maintain perspective. Growth control measures are not the only form of land use controls available to communities; they represent only one type of mechanism for controlling land use. Such measures are only a piece of a much larger framework by which communities can manage their land. The framework also includes general plans; traditional zoning, building and safety codes; parking requirements; arterial access requirements; publicly allocated space; and many other types of land use control; along with a plethora of procedural and financial restrictions, such as development impact fees. There are a number of wealthy communities that have very strong control over land without resorting to growth control types of

---

74. See David E. Dowall, *The Suburban Squeeze: Land Conversion and Regulation in the San Francisco Bay Area* (Berkeley: University of California Press, 1984). Dalton has also argued that a predominantly regulatory approach to plan implementation among California planning agencies yields enormous control to private property developers. See Dalton, "The Limits of Regulation."

75. See Baldassare, "Suburban Support for No-Growth Policies."

In California, there is no formal statewide growth policy.

measures (e.g., Palm Springs, Rancho Palos Verdes, San Marino). Part of the phenomenon of the growth control movement and the intense reaction against it is that these measures are *labelled* growth control, a label that incites emotional reactions on all sides of the issue. We suspect that if they were labeled 'zoning congruency' or 'infrastructure consistency' or some other more neutral phrase, there might have been a much less intense emotional reaction.

Refuting Common Perceptions about Growth Controls and Management

The results of our study contradict some of the common perceptions about the extent and types of growth controls enacted in California. We hope that the results will help refocus statewide, regional, and local policymakers on real issues and problems associated with growth and growth control in the state. For instance, the state legislature has previously shown considerable concern about the use of the initiative process for growth control, and yet most growth control is not enacted through the initiative process. Much concern has been raised about the enactment of controls in wealthy, white communities, and yet our data show no consistent racial or economic pattern in the enactment of controls. Many have accused cities that enact growth controls of trying to exclude affordable housing. Our study shows that cities that enact growth controls enact more affordable housing incentives than cities that do not, and that there is no difference between growth control and non–growth control jurisdictions in the extent to which they actually produce their fair share of affordable housing. However, overall the state remains far behind in the production of affordable housing. Finally, much concern has been raised about the imposition of housing caps and population caps, with statements about possible effects on the housing market in regions of the state. Our data show that the current pattern of enactment is unlikely to result in a reduction of regionwide housing production, but changes in that pattern of enactment should be monitored.

Broader Policy Implications

Growth management and growth controls have been enacted as a response mechanism for containing the negative effects of population growth and building activity.

In California, there is no formal statewide growth policy. A myriad of local, state, and federal policies constitute a de facto state policy. We have shown how the over nine hundred locally enacted growth measures now in effect in California are part of this de facto state growth policy. It is a complex web of policies; our study makes the web a little easier to view and comprehend. Once policymakers and citizens comprehend this implicit policy, it will be possible to judge its effects and effectiveness. It will then be possible to decide whether this 'policy' gives the state the future it wants or whether California needs a more formal state and regional growth policy. While all the evidence is not yet in, based on the results of this study, we lean in the direction of a more deliberate approach.

Growth management and growth controls have been enacted as a response mechanism for containing the negative effects of population growth and building activity. In the core and suburban areas of the metropolitan areas, measures have been enacted in response to concerns about increasing traffic congestion, poor air and water quality, limits on urban infrastructure, and fears that higher-density building will accelerate negative social conditions associated with high-density, crowded, old cities. In the exurban and rural areas, measures have been enacted in response to concern about the effects of population growth on urban sprawl, the increased infrastructure requirements of a spatially expanding population and its effects on air and water quality, the impacts of development on resources and agriculture, and other environmental concerns. Both cases have been a response to the rapid rate of population growth and spurts in building activity, and in most cases, these concerns are larger than the local jurisdictions that are enacting the measures.

Yet, at the same time, the evidence suggests that these measures have not been effective in reducing the rate of construction growth in California, at least for the time period measured in this study. Does this mean that enacting growth control or management measures is a useless exercise, designed more to demonstrate concern about the issue than to truly deal with the problems? We do not think so. But there *must* be some focused energy devoted to identifying those growth issues that *can* be successfully dealt with locally and those growth problems that must be recast in a larger regional context. Since local measures cannot really deal with all problems precipitating their enactment, there is a strong need for adjacent communities to coordinate their land use policies.

While there is a great deal of discussion about this issue in California, and there are several experimental efforts in this direction, at the moment there is no real subregional or regional government for most land use purposes. In California, the councils of government play a weak role and, with a few exceptions, county governments play no role in coordinating countywide land use policies outside the unincorporated areas. The federal government is only responsible for lands under its jurisdiction, which for the most part involve military lands, wilderness, and national parks and forests. Federal activities are exempt from local governmental review, as are state activities on state land.

All local land use authority is derived from the state, and, with some notable exceptions, the state has deferred to the home rule tradition. Agencies such as the State Lands Commission, state and regional Water Quality Control Boards, the State Department of Fish and Game, and the state and local Air Quality Districts all have some controls over local land use practices, but they are narrow in substantive authority. Furthermore, none of these agencies has participated in developing overall growth management plans with local governments or with each other; they simply regulate certain kinds of development through an independent permit process. Sometimes the permit requirements of one agency may be in direct conflict with the permit requirements of the local agency or another state or regional agency. That is now changing with regard to air quality and transportation; recent regulations by the South Coast Air Quality Management District specify planning requirements for local agencies and a still-evolving role for the district in regulating land use. Recent legislation has given county transportation commissions a new role in coordinating traffic congestion reduction plans that could affect local land use regulation. However, these regional and subregional agencies continue to be limited in substantive scope and remain institutionally incapable of re-

Since local measures cannot really deal with all problems precipitating their enactment, there is a strong need for adjacent communities to coordinate their land use policies.

These regional and subregional agencies continue to be limited in substantive scope and remain institutionally incapable of resolving conflicts between economic needs and environmental needs and among housing needs, job needs, and the timing and financing of infrastructure with development.

solving conflicts between economic needs and environmental needs and among housing needs, job needs, and the timing and financing of infrastructure with development.

Three Notable Exceptions for Comprehensive Planning

The state has taken a stronger and more comprehensive role in planning and regulating land use in limited areas because of overriding environmental concerns. The California Coastal Commission, the San Francisco Bay Conservation and Development Commission, and the Tahoe Regional Planning Agency are three such areas. The experience of the California Coastal Commission is instructive. The Coastal Act gives the Coastal Commission the authority to require local governments to submit comprehensive plans for review and approval. Once those plans are approved, all development must be consistent with the plan, or the local agency must seek approval for amendments. Local decisions may be appealed and overturned by the commission in parts of the coastal zone. The Coastal Commission has authority, within its area of jurisdiction, to require ports to submit master plans, state and private universities to submit long-range development plans, and other state agencies to submit master development plans and individual project plans for approval. Under the Federal Coastal Zone Management Act, the Coastal Commission is designated as the Coastal Zone Management agency for California. As such, all federal activities and licenses to private parties on federal lands and in federal waters off the California coastal zone require a certification or determination of consistency with the Coastal Act from the Coastal Commission. Thus, the Coastal Act is one of the only pieces of legislation that vests in one agency the ability to coordinate and approve the plans of local, state, and federal agencies for a particular area of interest.

The Coastal Commission blueprint was based on the framework and process established when the Bay Conservation and Development Commission (BCDC) was established in 1965 and made permanent in 1969. BCDC was designed to control the rapid filling of San Francisco Bay by establishing both a regional plan and a regional governing board to oversee the activities around the bay. BCDC regulates bay filling and dredging through a permit process for both governmental and private parties. It requires that projects be consistent with the overall plan for conservation and development of the bay. BCDC has twenty-seven members, representing federal and state agencies as well as local government and members of the public. It has been characterized as a "unique state/federal body that has worked reasonably well to carry out its mandate . . . . after twenty years as a permanent agency, BCDC is a fixture of the Bay Area's political and governmental landscape...the goals of 'saving the bay' have, to some extent been institutionalized."[76]

The Tahoe Regional Planning Agency (TRPA) oversees development within the entire Lake Tahoe Basin as a result of a bi-state compact between California and Nevada ratified by the U.S. Congress.

76. Senate Office of Research, *Does California Need A Policy to Manage Urban Growth? A Report from the Senate Urban Growth Policy Project* (June 1989), 43.

The agency is charged with issuing permits for all land use and shoreline development and is responsible "for insuring the environmental quality of the lake waters by creating a master plan for the entire Tahoe Basin."[77] Thus it combines the land use permitting and planning powers of BCDC and the Coastal Commission with the jurisdiction over water, air quality, soils, wildlife, recreation, and other resources. The history of TRPA has been rocky and fraught with controversy, lawsuits, and conflict. However, with relatively recent adoption of a new plan, and with the assistance of the California Tahoe Conservancy and the resolution of long-standing lawsuits, the agency now seems to be making headway towards a cleaner, healthier Lake Tahoe environment.

These three agencies have had varying levels of success in addressing some regional growth problems. Even so, all three have limitations as models for regional growth management in other areas of the state and the country. First, the jurisdictions of these agencies have been defined around resources rather than geographic and economic regions. TRPA's jurisdiction comes the closest to composing a true region, running across a state boundary and several counties to include a complete watershed and a single economic development area. In contrast, both the Coastal Commission and BCDC have long but linear jurisdictional responsibility, defined by a resource and running through highly urbanized regions that stretch many miles inland. Neither agency can implement a true regional plan.

Second, all three agencies were designed with limited objectives. For instance, while the Coastal Commission has broad authority over land use, it has, by statute, limited objectives focused on resource protection, recreation, and public access to the coast. Issues of unemployment, economic development, social services, fiscal soundness, and affordable housing are not within the mandate or jurisdiction of any of these agencies. Unlike a general-purpose government, none of these agencies has responsibility for funding any capital improvements or services.

Third, while BCDC and TRPA retain permanent permit authority within their jurisdictions, the Coastal Commission returns permit authority to local government after certifying a local coastal program. The commission has little authority to resolve land use conflicts between adjoining local governments. None of these agencies has input into the formation of new cities or annexations of land.

Fourth, one must question whether or not the problems of growth and the ineffectiveness of local government measures in solving them will have to become more apparent and more critical than they are now before local governments will be prepared either to give up permit authority to an agency like BCDC or TRPA or to submit to a plan certification process such as that required by the Coastal Act. Without the clear objective of "saving the coast," "saving the bay," or "saving the lake," there is little public support for new layers of government and much support for keeping government as accountable and close to local concerns as possible.

Given these circumstances, the state needs to formulate a framework for local jurisdictions, subregions, and regions to allocate and control the rate of growth, to coordinate financial investments in infra-

The state needs to formulate a framework for local jurisdictions, subregions, and regions to allocate and control the rate of growth, to coordinate financial investments in infrastructure, to meet development needs, and to protect air quality, water quality, and environmentally valuable lands. It needs to insure that this framework allows "regionalized decentralization."

---

77. Senate Office of Research, *Does California Need a Policy?*, 46.

structure, to meet development needs, and to protect air quality, water quality, and environmentally valuable lands. It needs to insure that this framework allows "regionalized decentralization"[78] so that, while government may need to be larger or at least better coordinated in responding to regional problems, it also becomes smaller and more accountable in responding to purely local problems. This need for greater local representation is even more critical in light of the current economic and racial segregation of poor and minority communities and the need to insure that their interests are represented adequately as regional issues are resolved.

Finally, there are limits to what California can do to solve its growth problems. As long as the state keeps growing at the rate that it has (over 700,000 people per year), a state growth policy framework and regional coordination of growth can only make more efficient use of land and resources, not insure that resources for further growth will be available.

---

78. "Regionalized decentralization" is a term coined by the late Donald G. Hagman to define a governmental structure whereby decisions with larger than local impacts would be made by regional governmental structures, or within regional guidelines, while decisions that were truly local in nature would be made at the neighborhood and smaller area level for greater accountability. This strategy calls for a government structure that is at the same time more regional and more local.

ABOUT THE AUTHORS

Madelyn J. Glickfeld has been involved in land use issues as an academic, a planning professional, and a citizen. Ms. Glickfeld has been a consulting planner since 1971 and formed her own consulting firm, MJG INC., in 1976. She has sixteen years of professional planning experience in a variety of assignments, specializing in land use and growth planning and policy.

Since 1983, Ms. Glickfeld has worked with the University of California at Los Angeles Public Policy Program, doing research and organizing conferences on a number of topics, including transfer of development rights, planning for environmentally sensitive areas, addressing the problems of antiquated subdivisions, and growth management and growth control issues.

From 1986 through 1989, Ms. Glickfeld focused her research activities on understanding the rapid increase in land use–related ballot measures in California and its implications for planning and development. She is a recognized expert in growth management and control trends and policy and has lectured throughout California on that topic. She co-authored research published in the UCLA Environmental Law Journal on trends in the use of the ballot for land use planning, and, with the UCLA Extension Public Policy Program, developed a major conference, "The Growth Controversy in California: Searching for Common Ground," which was attended by over 400 builders, realtors, environmentalists and community leaders trying to understand the varied perspectives on the growth issue.

Since 1988, with major support from the Lincoln Institute of Land Policy, the Urban Land Institute, and several other institutions, she has been working to monitor and analyze trends in state legislation and all local government measures related to growth management in California and has presented her work through lectures, conferences, and publication.

Since 1987, Ms. Glickfeld has been appointed to serve as a member of the California Coastal Commission, a statewide land use regulatory body for the coastal zone. She represents the commission on the Santa Monica Bay Management Conference, which is part of the National Estuaries Program. She is the commission's representative on the Santa Monica Mountains Conservancy. She has recently helped form the Santa Monica Mountains Enforcement Task Force, a voluntary regional organization focusing on reducing illegal development activities and promoting improved land use enforcement capabilities.

Ned Levine is Lecturer in Urban Planning at the Graduate School of Architecture and Urban Planning, University of California at Los Angeles, where he has been since 1980. He received a B.A. in psychology from the University of California at Berkeley in 1962 and a Ph.D. in social psychology from the London School of Economics in 1967. He taught in England at Brunel University from 1969 to 1973, in Turkey at the Middle East Technical University from 1967 to 1969, and at the Institute for Population Studies of Hacettepe University between 1973 and 1976.

At UCLA, Dr. Levine teaches courses on planning methodology. He developed the *HALLEY* population analysis program in 1983, among the first population projection programs for microcomputers. Dr. Levine plays a key role in the development of a geographic information system for the university.

With Madelyn Glickfeld, he has been studying growth management and control in California since 1988. Their first study was supported by a group of sponsors headed by the Lincoln Institute of Land Policy. They have recently started a second study to look at the relationships between growth control enactment and traffic congestion, water supply, urban limit lines, and spill-over effects onto adjacent jurisdictions.

Dr. Levine has over forty publications. His books include *Factors Affecting the Incidence of Bus Crime in Los Angeles* (with Martin Wachs) and *Population Policy Formation and Implementation in Turkey* (with Sunday Uner). He has also published articles in the *Journal of the American Planning Association, Journal of Architectural and Planning Research, Transportation Research, Journal of Developing Areas, Journal of Sound and Vibration, Sociology and Social Research, Social Forces, Human Relations,* and *Journal of Asian and African Studies.*

In recent years, many diverse agencies have utilized Dr. Levine's expertise in program development and project evaluation. Among these are the U.S. Urban Mass Transportation Administration; the U.S. Department of Energy; the South Coast Air Quality Management District; the Southern California Gas Company; the Cities of Los Angeles, Santa Monica, West Hollywood, and Anaheim; the National Association for the Advancement of Colored People Legal Defense Fund; the American Civil Liberties Union; the Kaiser Permanente medical group; and the Western Center for Law and Poverty.

Appendix A
SURVEY QUESTIONNAIRE AND CODEBOOK

League of California Cities
1400 K STREET • SACRAMENTO, CA 95814 • (916) 444-5790

California Cities
Work Together

Sacramento, CA.
November, 1988

TO: City Managers (City Clerks in Non-Manager Cities)

RE: **SURVEY ON LOCAL GROWTH CONTROL AND GROWTH MANAGEMENT MEASURES**

The League of California Cities is sending this survey on local growth control
and growth management measures to all cities in the state. The results will
provide a database that describes the scope and nature of growth control and
growth management measures being undertaken in local jurisdictions in
California. This data base will be used to assist individual cities now
considering growth control and growth management measures by providing
information on the types and impacts of such measures. This information will
also be considered by the League's Growth Control Task Force in developing
policies on growth control and growth management. In addition, we anticipate
that the next legislative session will be focused on growth control and growth
management restrictions.

This survey asks for information on all growth control or growth management
measures undertaken in your jurisdiction, whether adopted as an ordinance by
the city council or through the initiative ballot process. While people may
have different definitions of growth control and growth management measures,
for the purposes of this questionnaire such measures are those that control
the rate, intensity, type and distribution of development in the jurisdiction.

We would like you to identify measures that are applicable citywide, or have
an impact on the entire jurisdiction even though it may be limited to a
particular geographical area. Advisory measures, short-term restrictions
(such as a zoning moratorium to prepare a community plan), single site or
project restrictions which do not have a jurisdictionwide effect, or measures
which are no longer in effect should be excluded.

Only one survey per jurisdiction should be completed. Please have the staff
person who is the most knowledgeable on the purpose, content and impacts of
your city's growth control and growth management measures complete this
survey. In many jurisdictions, the Planning Director would probably be the
appropriate person.

Please fill out and return this survey even if you do not currently have any
growth control or growth management measures. It is extremely important that
every jurisdiction respond to this survey. We apologize for the length of
this survey, but please respond to all of the questions. Please return this
survey as soon as possible, but no later than December 30.

Thank you for your assistance. The results of this survey should be available
in February, 1989.

LEAGUE OF CALIFORNIA CITIES
SURVEY ON GROWTH CONTROL

RETURN BY DECEMBER 30.

GENERAL INFORMATION

1. NAME OF JURISDICTION: _____

2. NAME OF RESPONDENT: _____

3. TITLE OF RESPONDENT: _____

4. POPULATION: __not coded;replaced with standardized data__

5. GEOGRAPHIC LOCATION: not coded; replaced with standardized data

   Check one of the following:

   a._____ Northern Coastal   g._____ Central Inland
   b._____ Northern Foothill/Mountain h._____ Central Desert
   c._____ Northern Inland   i._____ Southern Coastal
   d._____ Northern Desert   j._____ Southern Foothill/Mountain
   e._____ Central Coastal   k._____ Southern Inland
   f._____ Central Foothill/Mountain   l._____ Southern Desert

6. DEVELOPMENT CHARACTER

   Check one of the following that describes the character of your city:

   a._____ Urban/Suburban   b._____ Rural

7. GROWTH DEMAND

   Check one of the following that best fits your city:

   a._____ There is a strong market demand for housing development in our
            jurisdiction.

   b._____ There is a strong market demand for commercial and industrial
            development in our jurisdiction.

   c._____ Both a. and b..

   d._____ There is a lack of a strong demand for growth in our
            jurisdiction.

   e._____ Other (Please Explain)_____

   _____.

8. PLANNING DOCUMENT STATUS

    Please check below all applicable statements regarding the status of your city's required planning documents.

    a._____ Our general plan is complete (i.e., includes all state mandated elements).
              Please note year of adoption:_____

    b._____ We are currently in the process of updating our general plan.

    c._____ We are currently in the process of updating one or more state mandated general plan elements.

not
coded d._____ Our general plan is incomplete or over 10 years old.

    e._____ We have asked for or received a general plan extension from the State Office of Planning and Research.

    f._____ We have adopted a general plan growth management element or are currently developing such an element.

not   g._____ Our housing element is complete and finally adopted.
coded   Please note year of adoption:_____.

not   h._____ We only have a draft housing element.
coded
not   i. According to the State Department of Housing, Community Development
coded   (HCD), our **adopted** housing element has been deemed:

           (1)_____ In compliance.   (2)_____ Out of compliance.

           (3)_____ Obsolete   (4)_____ No determination/unknown.

not   j. According to HCD, our **draft** housing element has been deemed:
coded
           (1)_____ In compliance.   (2)_____ Out of compliance.

           (3)_____ Obsolete.   (4)_____ No determination/unknown.

- -

II.   **RESIDENTIAL GROWTH CONTROL AND GROWTH MANAGEMENT MEASURES**

9. POPULATION GROWTH LIMITATIONS

    Does your city have a measure* which establishes a population growth limit or restricts the level of population growth for a given time frame (i.e., annual basis)?

    "Measure" includes initiatives adopted by the voters or regulatory ordinances adopted by the city council. It excludes resolutions or other policy statements.

a._____ YES   b._____ NO

If YES, adopted by (1)_____ initiative or (2)_____ ordinance.
                     (3)_____ year enacted.

10. HOUSING PERMIT LIMITATIONS

Does your city have a measure which restricts the total number of
permitted residential building permits in a given time frame (i.e., annual
basis) for:

a._____ YES   b._____ NO

If YES, applies to (1)_____ single family or (2)_____ multiple
                   family or (3)_____ both

If YES, total # of permitted units:(4) _____ per (5)_____.

If YES, adopted by (6)_____ initiative or (7)_____ ordinance.
                   (8)_____ year enacted.

11. HOUSING INFRASTRUCTURE REQUIREMENTS

Does your city have a measure which specifically requires
adequate service levels (i.e., road capacity/traffic congestion) or
service capacity (i.e., water, sewers, etc.) prior to or as a condition
of approval of a residential development?

a. _____ YES   b. _____ NO

If YES, adopted by (1)_____ initiative or (2)_____ ordinance.
                   (3)_____ year enacted.

12. HOUSING DENSITY AND LOCATIONAL RESTRICTIONS

Does your city have a measure which did any of the following (check all
applicable responses):

a._____ Reduced the permitted residential density by general plan
           amendment or rezoning.

           Applicable to: (1)_____ Entire City or (2)_____ Part of City
           Adopted by: (3)_____ initiative or (4)_____ ordinance.
           Year enacted: (5)_____.

b._____ Requires voter approval to increase residential densities.

           Applicable to: (1)_____ Entire City or (2)_____ Part of City
           Adopted by: (3)_____ initiative or (4)_____ ordinance.
           Year enacted: (5)_____.

c._____ Requires super majority council vote to increase residential
           densities.

       Applicable to: (1)_____ Entire City or (2)_____ Part of City
       Adopted by: (3)_____ initiative or (4)_____ ordinance.
       Year enacted: (5)_____ .

   d._____ Redesignated or rezoned land previously designated for
              residential development to agriculture or open space (i.e.,
              hillside or ridge preservation).

       Adopted by: (1)_____ initiative or (2)_____ ordinance.
                   (3) _____ year enacted.

IF YOU ANSWERED YES TO QUESTIONS 9, 10, OR 11, OR CHECKED A RESPONSE TO
QUESTION 12, PLEASE ANSWER THE FOLLOWING QUESTIONS 13 - 15. IF YOU ANSWERED
NO OR DID NOT CHECK A RESPONSE TO QUESTIONS 9-12, GO TO QUESTION 16.

13. PURPOSES OF RESIDENTIAL GROWTH CONTROL AND GROWTH MANAGEMENT MEASURES

    Please check all of the applicable purposes for all of your city's
    residential growth control or growth management measures as listed below:

    a._____ Air Quality
    b._____ Water Quality
    c._____ Agricultural Land Preservation
    d._____ Open Space/Ridgeline Preservation
    e._____ Limitation of Urban Sprawl
    f._____ Preservation of Sensitive Environmental Areas
    g._____ Reduction in Traffic Congestion
    h._____ Sewer Capacity Limitations
    i._____ Water Quantity Limitations
    j._____ Rapid Population/Housing Growth
    k._____ Quantity of High Density Housing Developments
    l._____ Quantity of Low Income Housing Developments
    m._____ Quality of Life Preservation
    n._____ Other: (please specify)_____
    o._____ Information not available
    p._____ Not applicable - no residential growth control or growth manage-
              ment measures

14. IMPACTS OF RESIDENTIAL GROWTH CONTROL AND GROWTH MANAGEMENT MEASURES

    Please check all of the applicable impacts of all of your city's
    residential growth control or growth management measures as listed below:

    a._____ Increase in housing costs above inflation rates.
    b._____ Reduction in the historical level of new housing development.
    c._____ Increase in average commute distances.
    d._____ Increase in traffic levels/congestion.
    e._____ Decrease in projected traffic levels/congestion.
    f._____ Reduction in projected population levels.
    g._____ Other. (Please specify):_____
    _____
    h._____ Information not available.

15. LOW-MODERATE INCOME HOUSING EXEMPTIONS

    Does your city exempt low and/or moderate income housing units (i.e.,
    affordable to families with an income of 120% or less of the median) from
    application of your residential growth control/growth management measures?

    a._____ YES.   b._____ NO.   c._____ Not applicable - no residential
                                          growth control or growth
                                          management measures.

16. LOW-MODERATE INCOME HOUSING INCENTIVES

    Does your city provide any incentives (i.e., density bonus, financial
    subsidies, etc.) for construction of low and/or moderate income housing
    units?

    a._____ YES.   b._____ NO.

    If YES, please specify: _____

    _____.

- -

III.   **COMMERCIAL AND/OR INDUSTRIAL GROWTH CONTROL AND GROWTH MANAGEMENT
        MEASURES**

17. SQUARE FOOTAGE LIMITATIONS

    Does your city have a measure that restricts the amount of square footage
    that can be built within a given time frame for:

    a. Commercial (i.e., retail and office): (1)_____ YES (2)_____ NO

    If YES, applicable to: (3) _____ Entire City or (4)_____ Part of City
    If YES, adopted by: (5)_____ initiative or (6)_____ ordinance
                         (7) _____ year enacted.

    b. Industrial (light industrial/warehouse): (1)____ YES (2)____ NO

    If YES, applicable to: (3) _____ Entire City or (4)_____ Part of City.
    If YES, adopted by: (5) _____ initiative or (6) _____ ordinance
                        (7) _____ year enacted.

18. COMMERCIAL/INDUSTRIAL INFRASTRUCTURE REQUIREMENTS

    Does your city have a measure that specifically requires adequate service
    levels (i.e., road capacity/traffic congestion) or service capacity (i.e.,
    water, sewer, etc.) prior to or as a condition of approval of commercial
    and/or industrial development?

    a._____ YES   b._____ NO

    If YES, adopted by: (1)_____ initiative or (2)_____ ordinance
                        (3)_____ year enacted.

19. COMMERCIAL/INDUSTRIAL LOCATIONAL RESTRICTIONS

    Does your city have a measure which redesignated or rezoned land
    previously designated for commercial and/or industrial development?

    a._____ YES   b._____ NO

    If YES, applicable to: (1) ____ Entire City or (2) ____ Part of City.
    If YES, adopted by: (3)_____ initiative or (4)_____ ordinance
                           (5)_____ year enacted.
    If YES, redesignated to: (6)_____ residential (7)_____ agriculture
                             (8)_____ other, Specify:_____

20. COMMERCIAL BUILDING HEIGHT LIMITATIONS

    Does your city have a measure adopted within the last 5 years, which
    restricts the permitted height of commercial/office buildings?

    a._____ YES   b._____ NO

    If YES, applicable to: (1)___ Entire City or (2)___ Part of City.

    If YES, adopted by: (3)_____ initiative or (4)_____ ordinance
                         (4)_____ year enacted.

IF YOU ANSWERED YES TO QUESTIONS 17, 18, 19 OR 20, PLEASE ANSWER THE FOLLOWING
QUESTIONS 21 - 22. IF YOU ANSWERED NO, GO TO QUESTION 23.

21. PURPOSES OF COMMERCIAL AND/OR INDUSTRIAL GROWTH CONTROL AND GROWTH
    MANAGEMENT MEASURES

    Please check all of the applicable purposes for all of your city's
    commercial/industrial growth control or growth management measures as
    listed below:

    a._____ Air Quality Preservation
    b._____ Water Quality Preservation
    c._____ Agricultural Land Preservation
    d._____ Open Space Preservation
    e._____ Limitation of Urban Sprawl
    f._____ Preservation of Sensitive Environmental Areas
    g._____ Reduction in Traffic Congestion
    h._____ Sewer Capacity Limitation
    i._____ Water Quantity Limitation
    j._____ Quality of Life Preservation
    k._____ Other (please specify):_____
    l._____ Information Not Available
    m._____ Not applicable -- no commercial/industrial growth control or
             growth management measures.

22. IMPACTS OF COMMERCIAL/INDUSTRIAL GROWTH AND GROWTH MANAGEMENT MEASURES

    Please check below all of the applicable impacts of all of your city's
    commercial/industrial growth control or growth management measures as
    listed below:

a._____ Increase in the average commute distance
b._____ Increase in traffic levels/congestion
c._____ Decrease in projected traffic levels/congestion
d._____ Reduction in the historical level of new commercial/industrial development.
e._____ Loss of projected new commercial, office or industrial developments/employers
f._____ Reduction in projected employment levels
g._____ Reductions in projected sales tax revenues
h._____ Reductions in projected property tax revenues
i._____ Increase in the historical level of residential development
j._____ Other (please specify):_____
k._____ Information not available
l._____ Not applicable -- no commercial/industrial growth control or growth management measures

23. JOBS/HOUSING BALANCE

Has your city enacted a policy or ordinance which specifies a desired or required ratio of the number of housing units per the number of jobs within a given area or within the entire city?

a._____ YES   b._____ NO

If YES, what is that ratio or percentage:_____

24. JOBS/HOUSING LINKAGE

Has your city enacted an ordinance to require commercial/industrial developers to pay in-lieu fees for housing development or to construct housing units as a condition of development approval?

a._____ YES   b._____ NO

- -

IV.   OTHER GROWTH CONTROL AND GROWTH MANAGEMENT MEASURES

25. URBAN LIMIT LINE/GREENBELT

Has your city established an urban limit line or greenbelt, other than the boundaries of your city, beyond which residential, commercial and/or industrial development is not currently permitted?

a._____ YES   b._____ NO

If YES, adopted by: (1)_____ initiative or (2)_____ ordinance.
                     (3)_____ year enacted.

26. OTHER MEASURES

Does your city have other existing or pending measures which fall under the definition of growth control or growth management which are not covered under the prior questions?

a._____ YES   b._____ NO

If YES, please describe: (1)_____

If YES, adopted by: (2)_____ initiative or (3)_____ ordinance or
                    (4)_____ pending and (5)_____ year enacted.

- -

**V.   MONITORING AND EVALUATION OF GROWTH CONTROL AND GROWTH MANAGEMENT
          MEASURES**

27. MONITORING BENEFITS AND IMPACTS

    Has your city established a program for monitoring or measuring the
    benefits and impacts of your growth control or growth management measures?

    a._____ YES   b._____ NO

28. EVALUATING BENEFITS AND IMPACTS

    Have any studies been conducted by the city or any other public or private
    agency or group to analyze the benefits and impacts of your growth control
    or growth management measures?

    a._____ YES   b._____ NO   c._____ Don't Know

    If YES, please list the titles and authors of these studies below:

    _____

    _____

    _____

- -

VI. GENERAL COMMENTS

29. Please use the space below to write any comments on growth control and
    growth management measures which were not included in the prior questions
    or any comments you may have on this survey.

    _____

    _____

    _____

    _____

    _____

_____

_____

_____

_____

_____

Please return this survey by **December 30** to:

    League of California Cities
    Attn: Sheryl Patterson
    1400 K Street, 4th Floor
    Sacramento, CA 95814

GROWTH.leg

Appendix B
FREQUENCIES OF QUESTIONNAIRE ITEMS

SURVEY (FREQUENCY TABULATION)

COUNT	CUM COUNT	PCT	CUM PCT	RESPONDE
443	443	100.0	100.0	1

COUNT	CUM COUNT	PCT	CUM PCT	URBAN$
146	146	49.2	49.2	LOS ANGELES
34	180	11.4	60.6	SACRAMENTO
18	198	6.1	66.7	SAN DIEGO
99	297	33.3	100.0	SF BAY AREA

COUNT	CUM COUNT	PCT	CUM PCT	REGION$
26	26	5.9	5.9	CENT COAST
19	45	4.3	10.2	CENT EAST
44	89	9.9	20.1	CENT INLAND
32	121	7.2	27.3	N CENTRAL
12	133	2.7	30.0	N COAST
9	142	2.0	32.1	NORTH EAST
34	176	7.7	39.7	SACRAMENTO
99	275	22.3	62.1	SF BAY AREA
128	403	28.9	91.0	SOUTH COAST
40	443	9.0	100.0	SOUTH INLAND

COUNT	CUM COUNT	PCT	CUM PCT	POPGROUP
96	96	21.7	21.7	Population<7500
65	161	14.7	36.3	7500<=Population<15000
78	239	17.6	54.0	15000<=Population<30000
96	335	21.7	75.6	30000<=Population<60000
71	406	16.0	91.6	60000<=Population<125000
22	428	5.0	96.6	125000<=Population<250000
9	437	2.0	98.6	250000<=Population<500000
6	443	1.4	100.0	500000<=Population

COUNT	CUM COUNT	PCT	CUM PCT	Q5
13	13	2.9	2.9	North Coast
98	111	22.1	25.1	San Francisco Bay
32	143	7.2	32.3	North Central
9	152	2.0	34.3	Northeastern
34	186	7.7	42.0	Stockton/Sacramento
36	222	8.1	50.1	Central Coastal
44	266	9.9	60.0	Central Inland
19	285	4.3	64.3	Central/Eastern
118	403	26.6	91.0	Southern Coastal
40	443	9.0	100.0	Southern Inland

SURVEY (Continued)

COUNT	CUM COUNT	PCT	CUM PCT	Q6
276	276	62.7	62.7	Urban/Suburban
154	430	35.0	97.7	Rural
6	436	1.4	99.1	Both 1 & 2
4	440	.9	100.0	Rural/Suburban

COUNT	CUM COUNT	PCT	CUM PCT	Q7$
110	110	24.9	24.9	Residential
9	119	2.0	26.9	Commercial/Industrial
241	360	54.5	81.4	Resident'l/commerc'l/Industr'l
54	414	12.2	93.7	No Demand
28	442	6.3	100.0	Other

COUNT	CUM COUNT	PCT	CUM PCT	Q8A
88	88	19.9	19.9	0
355	443	80.1	100.0	1

SURVEY (Continued)

COUNT	CUM COUNT	PCT	CUM PCT	Q8A_YEAR
1	1	.3	.3	1929
1	2	.3	.6	1962
2	4	.6	1.3	1964
1	5	.3	1.6	1965
2	7	.6	2.2	1967
1	8	.3	2.5	1968
1	9	.3	2.8	1969
3	12	.9	3.8	1970
4	16	1.3	5.0	1971
3	19	.9	5.9	1972
4	23	1.3	7.2	1973
7	30	2.2	9.4	1974
2	32	.6	10.0	1975
9	41	2.8	12.8	1976
6	47	1.9	14.7	1977
6	53	1.9	16.6	1978
7	60	2.2	18.8	1979
21	81	6.6	25.3	1980
15	96	4.7	30.0	1981
21	117	6.6	36.6	1982
23	140	7.2	43.8	1983
25	165	7.8	51.6	1984
25	190	7.8	59.4	1985
32	222	10.0	69.4	1986
24	246	7.5	76.9	1987
39	285	12.2	89.1	1988
7	292	2.2	91.3	1989
28	320	8.8	100.0	1999

COUNT	CUM COUNT	PCT	CUM PCT	Q8B
235	235	53.0	53.0	0
208	443	47.0	100.0	1

COUNT	CUM COUNT	PCT	CUM PCT	Q8C
251	251	56.7	56.7	0
192	443	43.3	100.0	1

COUNT	CUM COUNT	PCT	CUM PCT	Q8E
426	426	96.2	96.2	0
17	443	3.8	100.0	1

SURVEY (Continued)

COUNT	CUM COUNT	PCT	CUM PCT	Q8F	
456	456	89.9	89.9		0
51	507	10.1	100.0		1

COUNT	CUM COUNT	PCT	CUM PCT	Q9	
401	401	90.9	90.9		0
40	441	9.1	100.0		1

COUNT	CUM COUNT	PCT	CUM PCT	Q9_ADOPT$
15	15	38.5	38.5	Intiative
19	34	48.7	87.2	Ordinance
4	38	10.3	97.4	General Plan
1	39	2.6	100.0	Initiative/Ordinance

COUNT	CUM COUNT	PCT	CUM PCT	Q9_YEAR
1	1	2.7	2.7	1964
1	2	2.7	5.4	1975
1	3	2.7	8.1	1976
2	5	5.4	13.5	1977
2	7	5.4	18.9	1978
5	12	13.5	32.4	1979
3	15	8.1	40.5	1980
2	17	5.4	45.9	1981
1	18	2.7	48.6	1982
2	20	5.4	54.1	1984
2	22	5.4	59.5	1985
4	26	10.8	70.3	1986
3	29	8.1	78.4	1987
8	37	21.6	100.0	1988

SURVEY (Continued)

	CUM		CUM		
COUNT	COUNT	PCT	PCT	Q10	
50	50	100.0	100.0		1

	CUM		CUM	
COUNT	COUNT	PCT	PCT	Q10_FAMI$
2	2	4.0	4.0	Multi-Family
48	50	96.0	100.0	Single & Multi-Family

	CUM		CUM		
COUNT	COUNT	PCT	PCT	Q10_UNIT	
1	1	2.1	2.1		16
1	2	2.1	4.2		21
1	3	2.1	6.3		50
1	4	2.1	8.3		56
1	5	2.1	10.4		60
2	7	4.2	14.6		70
1	8	2.1	16.7		75
1	9	2.1	18.8		79
3	12	6.3	25.0		100
1	13	2.1	27.1		103
1	14	2.1	29.2		118
1	15	2.1	31.3		124
1	16	2.1	33.3		125
2	18	4.2	37.5		130
1	19	2.1	39.6		170
1	20	2.1	41.7		200
1	21	2.1	43.8		250
1	22	2.1	45.8		266
1	23	2.1	47.9		300
1	24	2.1	50.0		320
1	25	2.1	52.1		326
1	26	2.1	54.2		330
5	31	10.4	64.6		400
1	32	2.1	66.7		450
5	37	10.4	77.1		500
1	38	2.1	79.2		598
2	40	4.2	83.3		650
1	41	2.1	85.4		700
1	42	2.1	87.5		800
1	43	2.1	89.6		833
1	44	2.1	91.7		940
1	45	2.1	93.8		1200
1	46	2.1	95.8		1875
1	47	2.1	97.9		2140
1	48	2.1	100.0		8000

SURVEY (Continued)

COUNT	CUM COUNT	PCT	CUM PCT	Q10_ADOP$
13	13	27.7	27.7	Intiative
29	42	61.7	89.4	Ordinance
4	46	8.5	97.9	General Plan
1	47	2.1	100.0	Initiative/Ordinance

COUNT	CUM COUNT	PCT	CUM PCT	Q10_YEAR
2	2	4.9	4.9	1977
2	4	4.9	9.8	1978
5	9	12.2	22.0	1979
5	14	12.2	34.1	1980
5	19	12.2	46.3	1981
3	22	7.3	53.7	1982
2	24	4.9	58.5	1984
1	25	2.4	61.0	1985
3	28	7.3	68.3	1986
4	32	9.8	78.0	1987
9	41	22.0	100.0	1988

COUNT	CUM COUNT	PCT	CUM PCT	Q11
129	129	100.0	100.0	1

COUNT	CUM COUNT	PCT	CUM PCT	Q11_ADOP$
14	14	11.4	11.4	Intiative
86	100	69.9	81.3	Ordinance
21	121	17.1	98.4	General Plan
2	123	1.6	100.0	Initiative/Ordinance

SURVEY (Continued)

	CUM		CUM		
COUNT	COUNT	PCT	PCT	Q11_YEAR	
1	1	1.0	1.0		1956
1	2	1.0	2.0		1964
1	3	1.0	2.9		1965
2	5	2.0	4.9		1967
1	6	1.0	5.9		1969
1	7	1.0	6.9		1970
1	8	1.0	7.8		1972
1	9	1.0	8.8		1974
4	13	3.9	12.7		1975
5	18	4.9	17.6		1976
5	23	4.9	22.5		1978
2	25	2.0	24.5		1979
5	30	4.9	29.4		1980
5	35	4.9	34.3		1981
5	40	4.9	39.2		1982
2	42	2.0	41.2		1983
9	51	8.8	50.0		1984
2	53	2.0	52.0		1985
11	64	10.8	62.7		1986
7	71	6.9	69.6		1987
28	99	27.5	97.1		1988
1	100	1.0	98.0		1989
2	102	2.0	100.0		1999

	CUM		CUM		
COUNT	COUNT	PCT	PCT	Q12A	
322	322	72.7	72.7		0
121	443	27.3	100.0		1

	CUM		CUM	
COUNT	COUNT	PCT	PCT	Q12A_APP$
46	46	44.7	44.7	Entire City
57	103	55.3	100.0	Part of City

	CUM		CUM	
COUNT	COUNT	PCT	PCT	Q12A_ADO$
9	9	8.8	8.8	Intiative
77	86	75.5	84.3	Ordinance
15	101	14.7	99.0	General Plan
1	102	1.0	100.0	Initiative/Ordinance

SURVEY (Continued)

COUNT	CUM COUNT	PCT	CUM PCT	Q12A_YEA
1	1	.9	.9	1960
1	2	.9	1.8	1962
1	3	.9	2.7	1964
2	5	1.8	4.5	1974
2	7	1.8	6.3	1975
1	8	.9	7.2	1977
4	12	3.6	10.8	1978
4	16	3.6	14.4	1979
8	24	7.2	21.6	1980
4	28	3.6	25.2	1981
4	32	3.6	28.8	1982
1	33	.9	29.7	1983
4	37	3.6	33.3	1984
9	46	8.1	41.4	1985
13	59	11.7	53.2	1986
16	75	14.4	67.6	1987
32	107	28.8	96.4	1988
2	109	1.8	98.2	1989
2	111	1.8	100.0	1999

COUNT	CUM COUNT	PCT	CUM PCT	Q12B
424	424	95.7	95.7	0
19	443	4.3	100.0	1

COUNT	CUM COUNT	PCT	CUM PCT	Q12B_APP$
10	10	58.8	58.8	Entire City
7	17	41.2	100.0	Part of City

COUNT	CUM COUNT	PCT	CUM PCT	Q12B_ADO$
13	13	86.7	86.7	Intiative
2	15	13.3	100.0	Ordinance

SURVEY (Continued)

COUNT	CUM COUNT	PCT	CUM PCT	Q12B_YEA	
1	1	5.9	5.9		1907
1	2	5.9	11.8		1977
1	3	5.9	17.6		1979
2	5	11.8	29.4		1982
2	7	11.8	41.2		1984
1	8	5.9	47.1		1985
1	9	5.9	52.9		1986
3	12	17.6	70.6		1987
5	17	29.4	100.0		1988

COUNT	CUM COUNT	PCT	CUM PCT	Q12C	
432	432	97.5	97.5		0
11	443	2.5	100.0		1

COUNT	CUM COUNT	PCT	CUM PCT	Q12C_APP$
6	6	85.7	85.7	Entire City
1	7	14.3	100.0	Part of City

COUNT	CUM COUNT	PCT	CUM PCT	Q12C_ADO$
2	2	28.6	28.6	Intiative
5	7	71.4	100.0	Ordinance

COUNT	CUM COUNT	PCT	CUM PCT	Q12C_YEA	
1	1	16.7	16.7		1984
1	2	16.7	33.3		1986
4	6	66.7	100.0		1988

COUNT	CUM COUNT	PCT	CUM PCT	Q12D	
416	416	93.9	93.9		0
27	443	6.1	100.0		1

COUNT	CUM COUNT	PCT	CUM PCT	Q12D_ADO$
6	6	24.0	24.0	Intiative
15	21	60.0	84.0	Ordinance
4	25	16.0	100.0	General Plan

SURVEY (Continued)

COUNT	CUM COUNT	PCT	CUM PCT	Q12D_YEA	
1	1	4.2	4.2		1970
1	2	4.2	8.3		1976
2	4	8.3	16.7		1977
2	6	8.3	25.0		1979
1	7	4.2	29.2		1980
2	9	8.3	37.5		1981
2	11	8.3	45.8		1984
5	16	20.8	66.7		1985
3	19	12.5	79.2		1986
4	23	16.7	95.8		1987
1	24	4.2	100.0		1988

COUNT	CUM COUNT	PCT	CUM PCT	Q13A	
405	405	91.4	91.4		0
38	443	8.6	100.0		1

COUNT	CUM COUNT	PCT	CUM PCT	Q13B	
406	406	91.6	91.6		0
37	443	8.4	100.0		1

COUNT	CUM COUNT	PCT	CUM PCT	Q13C	
405	405	91.4	91.4		0
38	443	8.6	100.0		1

COUNT	CUM COUNT	PCT	CUM PCT	Q13D	
392	392	88.5	88.5		0
51	443	11.5	100.0		1

COUNT	CUM COUNT	PCT	CUM PCT	Q13E	
397	397	89.6	89.6		0
46	443	10.4	100.0		1

COUNT	CUM COUNT	PCT	CUM PCT	Q13F	
388	388	87.6	87.6		0
55	443	12.4	100.0		1

COUNT	CUM COUNT	PCT	CUM PCT	Q13G	
350	350	79.0	79.0		0
93	443	21.0	100.0		1

SURVEY (Continued)

	CUM		CUM		
COUNT	COUNT	PCT	PCT	Q13H	
361	361	81.5	81.5		0
82	443	18.5	100.0		1

	CUM		CUM		
COUNT	COUNT	PCT	PCT	Q13I	
380	380	85.8	85.8		0
63	443	14.2	100.0		1

	CUM		CUM		
COUNT	COUNT	PCT	PCT	Q13J	
392	392	88.5	88.5		0
51	443	11.5	100.0		1

	CUM		CUM		
COUNT	COUNT	PCT	PCT	Q13K	
408	408	92.1	92.1		0
35	443	7.9	100.0		1

	CUM		CUM		
COUNT	COUNT	PCT	PCT	Q13L	
429	429	96.8	96.8		0
14	443	3.2	100.0		1

	CUM		CUM		
COUNT	COUNT	PCT	PCT	Q13M	
345	345	77.9	77.9		0
98	443	22.1	100.0		1

	CUM		CUM		
COUNT	COUNT	PCT	PCT	Q13N	
385	385	86.9	86.9		0
58	443	13.1	100.0		1

	CUM		CUM		
COUNT	COUNT	PCT	PCT	Q13O	
442	442	99.8	99.8		0
1	443	.2	100.0		1

	CUM		CUM		
COUNT	COUNT	PCT	PCT	Q13P	
424	424	95.7	95.7		0
19	443	4.3	100.0		1

SURVEY (Continued)

COUNT	CUM COUNT	PCT	CUM PCT	Q13Q	
399	399	90.1	90.1		0
44	443	9.9	100.0		1

COUNT	CUM COUNT	PCT	CUM PCT	Q14A	
411	411	92.8	92.8		0
32	443	7.2	100.0		1

COUNT	CUM COUNT	PCT	CUM PCT	Q14B	
415	415	93.7	93.7		0
28	443	6.3	100.0		1

COUNT	CUM COUNT	PCT	CUM PCT	Q14C	
439	439	99.1	99.1		0
4	443	.9	100.0		1

COUNT	CUM COUNT	PCT	CUM PCT	Q14D	
438	438	98.9	98.9		0
5	443	1.1	100.0		1

COUNT	CUM COUNT	PCT	CUM PCT	Q14E	
414	414	93.5	93.5		0
29	443	6.5	100.0		1

COUNT	CUM COUNT	PCT	CUM PCT	Q14F	
400	400	90.3	90.3		0
43	443	9.7	100.0		1

COUNT	CUM COUNT	PCT	CUM PCT	Q14G	
411	411	92.8	92.8		0
32	443	7.2	100.0		1

COUNT	CUM COUNT	PCT	CUM PCT	Q14H	
380	380	85.8	85.8		0
63	443	14.2	100.0		1

SURVEY (Continued)

COUNT	CUM COUNT	PCT	CUM PCT	Q14I	
365	365	82.4	82.4		0
78	443	17.6	100.0		1

COUNT	CUM COUNT	PCT	CUM PCT	Q15	
400	400	94.1	94.1		0
25	425	5.9	100.0		1

COUNT	CUM COUNT	PCT	CUM PCT	Q16	
187	187	42.8	42.8		0
250	437	57.2	100.0		1

COUNT	CUM COUNT	PCT	CUM PCT	Q16_DENS	
254	254	57.3	57.3		0
189	443	42.7	100.0		1

COUNT	CUM COUNT	PCT	CUM PCT	Q16_BOND	
420	420	94.8	94.8		0
23	443	5.2	100.0		1

COUNT	CUM COUNT	PCT	CUM PCT	Q16_STRE	
426	426	96.2	96.2		0
17	443	3.8	100.0		1

COUNT	CUM COUNT	PCT	CUM PCT	Q16_GRAN	
432	432	97.5	97.5		0
11	443	2.5	100.0		1

COUNT	CUM COUNT	PCT	CUM PCT	Q16_SUBS	
402	402	90.7	90.7		0
41	443	9.3	100.0		1

COUNT	CUM COUNT	PCT	CUM PCT	Q16_REDE	
424	424	95.7	95.7		0
19	443	4.3	100.0		1

SURVEY (Continued)

COUNT	CUM COUNT	PCT	CUM PCT	Q16_WAIV	
425	425	95.9	95.9		0
18	443	4.1	100.0		1

COUNT	CUM COUNT	PCT	CUM PCT	Q16_OTHE	
397	397	89.6	89.6		0
46	443	10.4	100.0		1

COUNT	CUM COUNT	PCT	CUM PCT	Q17A	
427	427	96.8	96.8		0
14	441	3.2	100.0		1

COUNT	CUM COUNT	PCT	CUM PCT	Q17A_APP$
9	9	75.0	75.0	Entire City
3	12	25.0	100.0	Part of City

COUNT	CUM COUNT	PCT	CUM PCT	Q17A_ADO$
2	2	18.2	18.2	Intiative
7	9	63.6	81.8	Ordinance
2	11	18.2	100.0	General Plan

COUNT	CUM COUNT	PCT	CUM PCT	Q17A_YEA
1	1	9.1	9.1	1974
1	2	9.1	18.2	1980
1	3	9.1	27.3	1983
2	5	18.2	45.5	1986
1	6	9.1	54.5	1987
5	11	45.5	100.0	1988

COUNT	CUM COUNT	PCT	CUM PCT	Q17B	
408	408	96.9	96.9		0
13	421	3.1	100.0		1

COUNT	CUM COUNT	PCT	CUM PCT	Q17B_APP$
8	8	66.7	66.7	Entire City
4	12	33.3	100.0	Part of City

SURVEY (Continued)

COUNT	CUM COUNT	PCT	CUM PCT	Q17B_ADO$
10	10	90.9	90.9	Ordinance
1	11	9.1	100.0	General Plan

COUNT	CUM COUNT	PCT	CUM PCT	Q17B_YEA
1	1	10.0	10.0	1974
1	2	10.0	20.0	1980
2	4	20.0	40.0	1981
1	5	10.0	50.0	1983
2	7	20.0	70.0	1987
3	10	30.0	100.0	1988

COUNT	CUM COUNT	PCT	CUM PCT	Q18
333	333	75.5	75.5	0
108	441	24.5	100.0	1

COUNT	CUM COUNT	PCT	CUM PCT	Q18_ADOP$
11	11	10.9	10.9	Intiative
70	81	69.3	80.2	Ordinance
19	100	18.8	99.0	General Plan
1	101	1.0	100.0	Initiative/Ordinance

SURVEY (Continued)

COUNT	CUM COUNT	PCT	CUM PCT	Q18_YEAR
1	1	1.2	1.2	1964
1	2	1.2	2.5	1965
1	3	1.2	3.7	1967
1	4	1.2	4.9	1969
2	6	2.5	7.4	1970
1	7	1.2	8.6	1972
2	9	2.5	11.1	1974
3	12	3.7	14.8	1975
2	14	2.5	17.3	1976
2	16	2.5	19.8	1978
2	18	2.5	22.2	1979
4	22	4.9	27.2	1980
5	27	6.2	33.3	1981
3	30	3.7	37.0	1982
2	32	2.5	39.5	1983
5	37	6.2	45.7	1984
5	42	6.2	51.9	1985
11	53	13.6	65.4	1986
4	57	4.9	70.4	1987
21	78	25.9	96.3	1988
1	79	1.2	97.5	1989
2	81	2.5	100.0	1999

COUNT	CUM COUNT	PCT	CUM PCT	Q19
394	394	89.7	89.7	0
45	439	10.3	100.0	1

COUNT	CUM COUNT	PCT	CUM PCT	Q19_APPL$
9	9	20.9	20.9	Entire City
34	43	79.1	100.0	Part of City

COUNT	CUM COUNT	PCT	CUM PCT	Q19_ADOP$
5	5	12.5	12.5	Intiative
31	36	77.5	90.0	Ordinance
4	40	10.0	100.0	General Plan

COUNT	CUM COUNT	PCT	CUM PCT	Q19_REDE$
23	23	52.3	52.3	Residential
5	28	11.4	63.7	Agricultural
1	29	2.3	66.0	Residential/Agricultural
15	44	34.1	100.0	Other

SURVEY (Continued)

COUNT	CUM COUNT	PCT	CUM PCT	Q19_YEAR	
1	1	2.7	2.7		1960
1	2	2.7	5.4		1970
1	3	2.7	8.1		1975
2	5	5.4	13.5		1981
1	6	2.7	16.2		1983
4	10	10.8	27.0		1984
4	14	10.8	37.8		1985
4	18	10.8	48.6		1986
8	26	21.6	70.3		1987
7	33	18.9	89.2		1988
2	35	5.4	94.6		1989
2	37	5.4	100.0		1999

COUNT	CUM COUNT	PCT	CUM PCT	Q20	
325	325	74.4	74.4		0
112	437	25.6	100.0		1

COUNT	CUM COUNT	PCT	CUM PCT	Q20_APPL$
75	75	75.8	75.8	Entire City
24	99	24.2	100.0	Part of City

COUNT	CUM COUNT	PCT	CUM PCT	Q20_ADOP$
3	3	2.9	2.9	Intiative
97	100	92.4	95.2	Ordinance
5	105	4.8	100.0	General Plan

COUNT	CUM COUNT	PCT	CUM PCT	Q20_YEAR	
1	1	1.2	1.2		1954
1	2	1.2	2.4		1970
1	3	1.2	3.6		1975
1	4	1.2	4.8		1977
1	5	1.2	6.0		1979
1	6	1.2	7.1		1980
2	8	2.4	9.5		1982
4	12	4.8	14.3		1983
13	25	15.5	29.8		1984
9	34	10.7	40.5		1985
13	47	15.5	56.0		1986
21	68	25.0	81.0		1987
14	82	16.7	97.6		1988
1	83	1.2	98.8		1989
1	84	1.2	100.0		1999

SURVEY (Continued)

COUNT	CUM COUNT	PCT	CUM PCT	Q21A	
417	417	94.1	94.1		0
26	443	5.9	100.0		1

COUNT	CUM COUNT	PCT	CUM PCT	Q21B	
421	421	95.0	95.0		0
22	443	5.0	100.0		1

COUNT	CUM COUNT	PCT	CUM PCT	Q21C	
433	433	97.7	97.7		0
10	443	2.3	100.0		1

COUNT	CUM COUNT	PCT	CUM PCT	Q21D	
424	424	95.7	95.7		0
19	443	4.3	100.0		1

COUNT	CUM COUNT	PCT	CUM PCT	Q21E	
426	426	96.2	96.2		0
17	443	3.8	100.0		1

COUNT	CUM COUNT	PCT	CUM PCT	Q21F	
423	423	95.5	95.5		0
20	443	4.5	100.0		1

COUNT	CUM COUNT	PCT	CUM PCT	Q21G	
373	373	84.2	84.2		0
70	443	15.8	100.0		1

COUNT	CUM COUNT	PCT	CUM PCT	Q21H	
393	393	88.7	88.7		0
50	443	11.3	100.0		1

COUNT	CUM COUNT	PCT	CUM PCT	Q21I	
403	403	91.0	91.0		0
40	443	9.0	100.0		1

SURVEY (Continued)

	CUM		CUM		
COUNT	COUNT	PCT	PCT	Q21J	
378	378	85.3	85.3		0
65	443	14.7	100.0		1

	CUM		CUM		
COUNT	COUNT	PCT	PCT	Q21K	
395	395	89.2	89.2		0
48	443	10.8	100.0		1

	CUM		CUM		
COUNT	COUNT	PCT	PCT	Q21L	
440	440	99.3	99.3		0
3	443	.7	100.0		1

	CUM		CUM		
COUNT	COUNT	PCT	PCT	Q21M	
414	414	93.5	93.5		0
29	443	6.5	100.0		1

	CUM		CUM		
COUNT	COUNT	PCT	PCT	Q21N	
414	414	93.5	93.5		0
29	443	6.5	100.0		1

	CUM		CUM		
COUNT	COUNT	PCT	PCT	Q22A	
442	442	99.8	99.8		0
1	443	.2	100.0		1

	CUM		CUM		
COUNT	COUNT	PCT	PCT	Q22B	
434	434	98.0	98.0		0
9	443	2.0	100.0		1

	CUM		CUM		
COUNT	COUNT	PCT	PCT	Q22C	
417	417	94.1	94.1		0
26	443	5.9	100.0		1

	CUM		CUM		
COUNT	COUNT	PCT	PCT	Q22D	
432	432	97.5	97.5		0
11	443	2.5	100.0		1

SURVEY (Continued)

	CUM		CUM		
COUNT	COUNT	PCT	PCT	Q22E	
431	431	97.3	97.3		0
12	443	2.7	100.0		1

	CUM		CUM		
COUNT	COUNT	PCT	PCT	Q22F	
430	430	97.1	97.1		0
13	443	2.9	100.0		1

	CUM		CUM		
COUNT	COUNT	PCT	PCT	Q22G	
437	437	98.6	98.6		0
6	443	1.4	100.0		1

	CUM		CUM		
COUNT	COUNT	PCT	PCT	Q22H	
436	436	98.4	98.4		0
7	443	1.6	100.0		1

	CUM		CUM		
COUNT	COUNT	PCT	PCT	Q22I	
438	438	98.9	98.9		0
5	443	1.1	100.0		1

	CUM		CUM		
COUNT	COUNT	PCT	PCT	Q22J	
420	420	94.8	94.8		0
23	443	5.2	100.0		1

	CUM		CUM		
COUNT	COUNT	PCT	PCT	Q22K	
408	408	92.1	92.1		0
35	443	7.9	100.0		1

	CUM		CUM		
COUNT	COUNT	PCT	PCT	Q22L	
398	398	89.8	89.8		0
45	443	10.2	100.0		1

	CUM		CUM		
COUNT	COUNT	PCT	PCT	Q22M	
388	388	87.6	87.6		0
55	443	12.4	100.0		1

SURVEY (Continued)

	CUM		CUM		
COUNT	COUNT	PCT	PCT	Q23	
418	418	96.3	96.3		0
16	434	3.7	100.0		1

	CUM		CUM		
COUNT	COUNT	PCT	PCT	Q24	
425	425	96.8	96.8		0
14	439	3.2	100.0		1

	CUM		CUM		
COUNT	COUNT	PCT	PCT	Q25	
363	363	82.1	82.1		0
79	442	17.9	100.0		1

	CUM		CUM	
COUNT	COUNT	PCT	PCT	Q25_ADOP$
4	4	5.5	5.5	Intiative
34	38	46.6	52.1	Ordinance
35	73	47.9	100.0	General Plan

	CUM		CUM		
COUNT	COUNT	PCT	PCT	Q25_YEAR	
1	1	1.7	1.7		1929
1	2	1.7	3.4		1970
6	8	10.2	13.6		1973
3	11	5.1	18.6		1975
2	13	3.4	22.0		1976
1	14	1.7	23.7		1977
2	16	3.4	27.1		1978
4	20	6.8	33.9		1979
2	22	3.4	37.3		1980
5	27	8.5	45.8		1981
5	32	8.5	54.2		1982
3	35	5.1	59.3		1983
4	39	6.8	66.1		1984
5	44	8.5	74.6		1985
1	45	1.7	76.3		1986
6	51	10.2	86.4		1987
5	56	8.5	94.9		1988
3	59	5.1	100.0		1999

	CUM		CUM		
COUNT	COUNT	PCT	PCT	Q26	
353	353	80.0	80.0		0
88	441	20.0	100.0		1

SURVEY (Continued)

COUNT	CUM COUNT	PCT	CUM PCT	Q26_ADOP$
10	10	16.9	16.9	Intiative
21	31	35.6	52.5	Ordinance
26	57	44.1	96.6	General Plan
2	59	3.4	100.0	Initiative/Ordinance

COUNT	CUM COUNT	PCT	CUM PCT	Q26_YEAR
1	1	5.3	5.3	1976
1	2	5.3	10.5	1977
1	3	5.3	15.8	1979
1	4	5.3	21.1	1985
5	9	26.3	47.4	1986
3	12	15.8	63.2	1987
5	17	26.3	89.5	1988
1	18	5.3	94.7	1989
1	19	5.3	100.0	1999

COUNT	CUM COUNT	PCT	CUM PCT	Q26_PEND	
389	389	87.8	87.8		0
54	443	12.2	100.0		1

COUNT	CUM COUNT	PCT	CUM PCT	Q27	
395	395	92.3	92.3		0
33	428	7.7	100.0		1

COUNT	CUM COUNT	PCT	CUM PCT	Q28	
334	334	78.8	78.8		0
34	368	8.0	86.8		1
56	424	13.2	100.0		2

Appendix C
DISTRIBUTION OF MEASURES IN CALIFORNIA CITIES AND COUNTIES

GEOGRAPHICAL LOCATION	COUNTY	CITY	Q8F	Q9	Q10	Q11	Q12A	Q12B	Q12C	Q12D	Q17A	Q17B	Q18	Q19	Q20	Q25	Q26	TOTAL	Q26 PEND	AVG NO OF MEAS.	% W/ MEAS.
CENT COAST	MONTEREY		0	0	0	1	1	0	0	0	0	0	1	0	0	1	1	5			
		CARMEL	0	0	0	1	1	0	0	0	0	0	1	0	1	1	0	5			
		DEL REY OAKS	0	0	0	0	0	0	0	0	0	0	0	0	0	0	0	0			
		GONZALES	0	0	0	0	1	0	0	0	0	0	0	0	0	0	0	1			
		GREENFIELD	0	0	0	1	0	0	0	0	0	0	1	0	0	0	0	2			
		KING CITY	0	0	0	0	0	0	0	0	0	0	0	0	1	0	0	1			
		MARINA	0	0	0	0	1	0	0	0	0	0	0	0	0	0	1	2			
		MONTEREY	1	0	0	1	0	1	0	0	0	0	0	0	1	0	0	4			
		PACIFIC GROV	0	0	0	1	1	0	0	0	0	0	1	0	0	0	0	3			
		SALINAS	0	0	0	1	1	0	0	0	0	0	1	0	0	1	0	4			
		SEASIDE	0	0	1	1	1	0	0	0	0	0	0	0	0	0	0	3			
		SOLEDAD	0	0	0	0	0	0	0	0	0	0	0			0	1	1			
	COUNTY TOTAL		1	0	1	7	7	1	0	0	0	0	5	0	3	3	3	31	0	2.58	91.7%
	SAN LUIS OBI		0	0	1	0	1	0	0	1	0	0	0	0	0	0	0	3	1		
		ATASCADERO	0	0	0	0	1	0	0	0	0	0	0	0	0	1	0	2			
		GROVER CITY	1	0	0	0	0	0	0	0	0	0	0	0	0	0	0	1			
		MORRO BAY	0	1	1	1	1	0	0	0	0	0	1	0	0	1	0	6			
		PASO ROBLES	0	0	0	0	0	0	0	0	0	0	0	0	0	0	0	0			
		PISMO BEACH	1	0	0	0	0	0	0	0	0	0	0	0	0	0	1	2			
		SAN LUIS OBI	1	1	1	0	1	0	0	1	1	1	0	0	1	1	0	9	1		
	COUNTY TOTAL		3	2	3	1	4	0	0	2	1	1	1	0	1	3	1	23	2	3.29	85.7%
	SANTA BARBAR		1	0	1	1	1	0	0	0	0	0	1	0	0	1	0	6	1		
		CARPINTERIA	0	0	0	1	0	0	0	0	0	0	1	0	0	1	0	3			
		GUADALUPE	0	0	0	0	0	0	0	0	0	0	0	0	0	0	0	0			
		LOMPOC	0	0	0	1	0	0	1	0	0	0	1	0	0	0	0	3			
		SANTA BARBAR	0	1	0	0	1	0	1	0	0	0	0	0	0	0	0	3	1		
		SANTA MARIA	0	0	0	0	0	0	0	0	0	0	0	0	1	1	0	2			
		SOLVANG	0	0	0	0	0	0	0	0	0	0	1	1	1	0	0	3	1		
	COUNTY TOTAL		1	1	1	3	2	0	2	0	0	0	4	1	2	3	0	20	3	2.86	85.7%
	REGION TOTAL		5	3	5	11	13	1	2	2	1	1	10	1	6	4	0	74	5		

RESIDENTIAL, COMMERCIAL AND OTHER GROWTH CONTROL MEASURES

GEOGRAPHICAL LOCATION	COUNTY	CITY	RESIDENTIAL, COMMERCIAL AND OTHER GROWTH CONTROL MEASURES															TOTAL	Q26 PEND	AVG NO OF MEAS.	% W/ MEAS.
			Q8F	Q9	Q10	Q11	Q12A	Q12B	Q12C	Q12D	Q17A	Q17B	Q18	Q19	Q20	Q25	Q26				
CENT EAST	ALPINE		0	0	0	1	0	0	0	0	0	0	1	0	1	0	0	3			
	COUNTY TOTAL		0	0	0	1	0	0	0	0	0	0	1	0	1	0	0	3	0	3.00	100.0%
	AMADOR		0	0	0	0	1	0	0	0	0	0	0	0	0	0	0	1			
		AMADOR	0	0	0	1	0	0	0	0	0	0	1	0	0	0	0	2			
		IONE	0	0	0	0	0	0	0	0	0	0	0	0	0	0	0	0			
		JACKSON	0	0	0	0	0	0	0	0	0	0	0	0	0	0	0	0			
		PLYMOUTH	0	0	0	1	0	0	0	0	0	0	1	0	1	0	1	4			
		SUTTER CREEK	0	0	0	0	0	0	0	0	0	0	0	0	1	0	0	1			
	COUNTY TOTAL		0	0	0	2	1	0	0	0	0	0	2	0	2	0	1	8	0	1.33	66.7%
	CALAVERAS		0	0	0	1	1	0	0	0	0	0	1	0	1	0	0	4			
		ANGELS CAMP	0	0	0	0	0	0	0	0	0	0	1	0	1	0	0	2			
	COUNTY TOTAL		0	0	0	1	1	0	0	0	0	0	2	0	2	0	0	6	0	3.00	100.0%
	INYO		0	0	0	0	0	0	0	0	0	0	0	0	0	0	0	0			
		BISHOP	0	0	0	0	0	0	0	0	0	0	0	0	1	0	0	1			
	COUNTY TOTAL		0	0	0	0	0	0	0	0	0	0	0	0	1	0	0	1	0	0.50	50.0%
	MADERA		0	0	0	0	1	0	0	0	0	0	0	0	0	0	0	1			
		CHOWCHILLA	0	0	0	1	0	0	0	0	0	0	1	0	0	0	0	2			
		MADERA	0	0	0	0	0	0	0	0	0	0	0	0	0	0	0	0			
	COUNTY TOTAL		0	0	0	1	1	0	0	0	0	0	1	0	0	0	0	3	0	1.00	66.7%
	MARIPOSA		0	0	0	1	0	0	0	0	0	0	1	0	0	0	0	2			
	COUNTY TOTAL		0	0	0	1	0	0	0	0	0	0	1	0	0	0	0	2	0	2.00	100.0%
	MONO		0	0	0	0	0	0	0	0	0	0	0	0	1	0	0	1	1		
		MAMMOTH LAKE	0	0	0	1	0	0	0	0	0	0	0	0	1	0	0	2	1		
	COUNTY TOTAL		0	0	0	1	0	0	0	0	0	0	0	0	2	0	0	3	2	1.50	100.0%

GEOGRAPHICAL LOCATION	COUNTY	CITY	RESIDENTIAL, COMMERCIAL AND OTHER GROWTH CONTROL MEASURES															TOTAL	Q26 PEND	AVG NO OF MEAS.	% W/ MEAS.
			Q8F	Q9	Q10	Q11	Q12A	Q12B	Q12C	Q12D	Q17A	Q17B	Q18	Q19	Q20	Q25	Q26				
	TUOLUMNE		0	0	0	1	1	0	0	0	0	0	1	0	0	0	0	3			
		SONORA	0	0	0	0	0	0	0	0	0	0	0	0	0	0	0	0			
	COUNTY TOTAL		0	0	0	1	1	0	0	0	0	0	1	0	0	0	0	3	0	1.50	50.0%
	REGION TOTAL		0	0	0	8	4	0	0	0	0	0	8	0	8	0	1	29	2		
CENT INLAND	FRESNO		0	0	0	1	0	0	0	0	0	0	0	0	0	1	1	3			
		CLOVIS	0	0	0	0	0	0	0	0	0	0	0	0	0	1	0	1			
		COALINGA	0	0	0	0	0	0	0	0	0	0	0	0	0	0	0	0	1		
		FOWLER	0	0	0	0	1	0	0	0	0	0	0	0	0	0	0	1			
		FRESNO	1	0	0	1	1	0	0	0	0	0	1	1	1	1	0	7			
		HURON	0	0	0	1	0	0	1	0	0	0	0	0	0	0	0	2			
		KERMAN	0	0	0	0	1	0	0	0	0	0	0	0	1	0	0	2			
		KINGSBURG	0	0	0	1	0	0	0	0	0	0	0	0	0	0	0	1			
		MENDOTA	0	0	0	0	0	0	0	0	0	0	0	0	0	0	0	0			
		ORANGE COVE	0	0	0	1	0	0	0	0	0	0	0	0	0	0	0	1			
		REEDLEY	0	0	0	1	0	0	0	0	0	0	1	0	0	1	1	4			
		SAN JOAQUIN	0	0	0	0	0	0	0	0	0	0	0	0	0	0	0	0			
		SANGER	0	0	0	1	0	0	0	0	0	0	1	0	0	0	0	2			
	COUNTY TOTAL		1	0	0	7	3	0	1	0	0	0	3	1	2	4	2	24	1	1.85	76.9%
	KERN		0	0	0	1	1	0	0	1	0	0	1	0	1	1	0	6			
		ARVIN	0	0	0	0	0	0	0	0	0	0	0	0	0	0	0	0	1		
		BAKERSFIELD	0	0	0	0	0	0	0	0	0	0	0	0	0	0	0	0			
		CALIFORNIA C	0	0	0	1	0	0	0	0	0	0	1	0	1	1	0	4			
		MCFARLAND	0	0	0	0	0	0	0	0	0	0	0	0	0	0	0	0			
		RIDGECREST	0	0	0	1	0	0	0	0	0	0	1	0	0	0	0	2			
		SHAFTER	0	0	0	0	0	0	0	0	0	0	0	0	0	0	0	0			
		TAFT	0	0	0	0	0	0	0	0	0	0	0	0	0	0	0	0			
		WASCO	0	0	0	1	0	0	0	0	0	0	1	0	1	0	0	3	1		
	COUNTY TOTAL		0	0	0	4	1	0	0	1	0	0	4	0	3	2	0	15	2	1.67	44.4%
	KINGS		0	0	0	1	0	0	0	0	0	0	1	0	0	1	0	3			
		AVENAL	0	0	0	0	0	0	0	0	0	0	0	0	0	0	0	0			
		CORCORAN	0	0	0	0	0	0	0	0	0	0	0	0	1	0	0	1			
		HANFORD	0	0	0	0	0	0	0	0	0	0	0	0	0	0	0	0			
		LEMOORE	0	0	0	0	0	0	0	0	0	0	0	0	0	0	0	0			
	COUNTY TOTAL		0	0	0	1	0	0	0	0	0	0	1	0	1	1	0	4	0	0.80	40.0%

GEOGRAPHICAL LOCATION	COUNTY	CITY	RESIDENTIAL, COMMERCIAL AND OTHER GROWTH CONTROL MEASURES														TOTAL	Q26 PEND	AVG NO OF MEAS.	% W/ MEAS.
			Q8F	Q9	Q10	Q11	Q12A	Q12B	Q12C	Q12D	Q17A	Q17B	Q18	Q19	Q20	Q25	Q26				
	MERCED		0	0	0	1	0	0	0	0	0	0	1	0	0	1	0	3			
		DOS PALOS	0	0	0	0	0	0	0	0	0	0	0	0	0	0	0	0			
		GUSTINE	0	0	0	0	0	0	0	0	0	0	0	0	0	0	0	0			
		LIVINGSTON	0	0	0	0	0	0	0	0	0	0	0	0	0	1	0	1			
		LOS BANOS	0	0	0		0	0	0	0	0	0		0	1	1	0	2			
		MERCED	0	0	0	0	0	0	0	0	0	0	0	0	0	1	0	1			
	COUNTY TOTAL		0	0	0	1	0	0	0	0	0	0	1	0	1	4	0	7	0	1.17	66.7%
	SAN BENITO		0	0	0	0	0	0	0	0	0	0	0	0	0	0	0	0			
		HOLLISTER	1	1	1	1	0	0	0	0	0	0	0	0	0	1	0	5			
		SAN JUAN BAU	1	1	1	1	1	0	1	0	0	0	1	1	0	1	0	9	1		
	COUNTY TOTAL		2	2	2	2	1	0	1	0	0	0	1	1	0	2	0	14	1	4.67	66.7%
	TULARE		0	0	0	0	0	0	0	1	0	0	0	0	0	1	0	2			
		DINUBA	0	0	0	1	0	0	0	0	0	0	0	0	0	0	0	1			
		EXETER	0	0	0	0	0	0	0	0	0	0	0	0	0	1	0	1			
		FARMERSVILLE	0	0	0	1	0	0	0	0	0	0	1	0	1	0	0	3			
		PORTERVILLE	0	0	0	0	0	0	0	0	0	0	0	0	0	0	0	0			
		TULARE	0	0	0	0	0	0	0	0	0	0	0	0	0	1	0	1			
		VISALIA	0	0	0	0	1	0	0	1	0	0	0	0	0	1	0	3			
		WOODLAKE	0	0	0	1	0	0	0	0	0	0	1	0	0	1	0	3			
	COUNTY TOTAL		0	0	0	3	1	0	0	2	0	0	2	0	1	5	0	14	0	1.75	87.5%
	REGION TOTAL		3	2	2	18	6	0	2	3	0	0	12	2	8	18	2	78	4		

GEOGRAPHICAL LOCATION	COUNTY	CITY	RESIDENTIAL, COMMERCIAL AND OTHER GROWTH CONTROL MEASURES															TOTAL	Q26 PEND	AVG NO OF MEAS.	% W/ MEAS.
			Q8F	Q9	Q10	Q11	Q12A	Q12B	Q12C	Q12D	Q17A	Q17B	Q18	Q19	Q20	Q25	Q26				
N CENTRAL	BUTTE		1	0	0	0	0	0	0	0	0	0	0	0	0	1	0	2	1		
		CHICO	0	0	0	0	1	0	0	0	0		0	0	0	1	0	2			
		GRIDLEY	0	0	0	0	1	0	0	1	0	0	1	1	1	1	0	6			
		PARADISE	0	0	0	0	0	0	0	0	0	0	0	0	1	0	0	1			
	COUNTY TOTAL		1	0	0	0	2	0	0	1	0	0	1	1	2	3	0	11	1	2.75	100.0%
	COLUSA		0	0	0	0	0	0	0	0	0		0	0	0	0	0	0			
		COLUSA	0	0	0	0	0	0	0	0	0	0	0	0	0	0	0	0			
	COUNTY TOTAL		0	0	0	0	0	0	0	0	0	0	0	0	0	0	0	0	0	0.00	0.0%
	GLENN		0	0	0	0	0	0	0	0	0		0	0	1	0	0	1			
		ORLAND	0	0	0	1	0	0	0	0	0	0	1	0	0	0	0	2			
		WILLOWS	0	0	0	0	0	0	0	0	0	0	0	0	0	0	0	0			
	COUNTY TOTAL		0	0	0	1	0	0	0	0	0	0	1	0	1	0	0	3	0	1.00	66.7%
	LAKE		0	0	0	0	0	0	0	0	0		0	0	0	0	0	0			
		CLEARLAKE	0	0	0	0	0	0	0	0	0	0	1	0	1	0	0	2			
	COUNTY TOTAL		0	0	0	0	0	0	0	0	0	0	1	0	1	0	0	2	0	1.00	50.0%
	SHASTA		0	0	0	0	0	0	0	0	0		0	0	0	0	0	0			
		ANDERSON	0	0	0	0	0	0	0	0	0	0	0	0	1	0	0	1			
		REDDING	0	0	0	0	0	0	0	0	0	0	0	0	0	0	0	0			
	COUNTY TOTAL		0	0	0	0	0	0	0	0	0	0	0	0	1	0	0	1	0	0.33	33.3%
	SISKIYOU		0	0	0	1	1	0	0	0	0		1	0	0	0	0	3			
		DUNSMUIR	0	0	0	0	0	0	0	0	0	0	0	0	0	0	0	0			
		ETNA	0	0	0	0	0	0	0	0	0	0	0	0	0	0	0	0			
		FORT JONES	0	0	0	0	0	0	0	0	0		0	0	0	0	0	0			
		MONTAGUE	0	0	0	0	0	0	0	0	0	0	0	0	0	0	0	0			
		MT. SHASTA	0	0	0	1	0	0	0	0	0	0	1	0	0	0	0	2			
		WEED	0	0	0	0	0	0	0	0	0	0	0	0	0	0	0	0			
		YREKA	0	0	0	1	0	0	0	0	0	0	1	0	0	0	0	2			
	COUNTY TOTAL		0	0	0	3	1	0	0	0	0	0	3	0	0	0	0	7	0	0.88	37.5%

GEOGRAPHICAL LOCATION	COUNTY	CITY	Q8F	Q9	Q10	Q11	Q12A	Q12B	Q12C	Q12D	Q17A	Q17B	Q18	Q19	Q20	Q25	Q26	TOTAL	Q26 PEND	AVG NO OF MEAS.	% W/ MEAS.
	SUTTER		0	0	0	0	0	0	0	0	0	0	0	0	0	1	0	1			
		YUBA CITY	0	0	0	0	0	0	0	0	0	0	0	0	0	0	0	0			
	COUNTY TOTAL		0	0	0	0	0	0	0	0	0	0	0	0	0	1	0	1	0	0.50	50.0%
	TEHAMA		0	0	0	0	0	0	0	0	0	0	0	0	1	0	0	1			
		CORNING	0	0	0	0	0	0	0	0	0	0	0	0	0	0	0	0			
		RED BLUFF	0	0	0	0	0	0	0	0	0	0	0	0	0	0	0	0			
		TEHAMA	0	0	0	0	0	0	0	0	0	0	0	0	0	0	0	0			
	COUNTY TOTAL		0	0	0	0	0	0	0	0	0	0	0	0	1	0	0	1	0	0.25	25.0%
	TRINITY		0	0	0	0	0	0	0	0	0	0	0	0	0	0	0	0			
	COUNTY TOTAL		0	0	0	0	0	0	0	0	0	0	0	0	0	0	0	0	0	0.00	0.0%
	YUBA		0	0	0	0	0	0	0	0	0	0	0	0	0	0	0	0			
		MARYSVILLE	0	0	0	0	0	0	0	0	0		0	0	0	0	0	0			
		WHEATLAND	0	0	0	0	0	0	0	0	0	0	0	0	0	0	0	0			
	COUNTY TOTAL		0	0	0	0	0	0	0	0	0	0	0	0	0	0	0	0	0	0.00	0.0%
	REGION TOTAL		1	0	0	4	3	0	0	1	0	0	6	1	6	4	0	26	1		
N COAST	DEL NORTE		0	0	0	0	0	0	0	0	0	0	0	0	0	1	0	1			
		CRESCENT CIT	0	0	0	0	0	0	0	0	0	0	0	0	0	0	0	0			
	COUNTY TOTAL		0	0	0	0	0	0	0	0	0	0	0	0	0	1	0	1	0	0.50	50.0%
	HUMBOLDT		0	0	0	0	0	0	0	0	0	0	0	0	0	1	0	1			
		BLUE LAKE	0	0	0	0	0	0	0	0	0	0	0	0	0	0	0	0			
		EUREKA	0	0	0	0	0	0	0	0	0	0	0	0	0	0	0	0			
		FORTUNA	0	0	0	1	0	0	0	0	0	0	1	0	0	0	0	2			
		TRINIDAD	0	0	0	1	0	0	0	0	0	0	0	0	1	0	0	2			
	COUNTY TOTAL		0	0	0	2	0	0	0	0	0	0	1	0	1	1	0	5	0	1.00	60.0%

RESIDENTIAL, COMMERCIAL AND OTHER GROWTH CONTROL MEASURES

GEOGRAPHICAL LOCATION	COUNTY	CITY	Q8F	Q9	Q10	Q11	Q12A	Q12B	Q12C	Q12D	Q17A	Q17B	Q18	Q19	Q20	Q25	Q26	TOTAL	Q26 PEND	AVG NO OF MEAS.	% W/ MEAS.
	MENDOCINO		0	0	0	0	1	0	0	0	0		0	0	0	1	0	2			
		FORT BRAGG	0	0	0	0	0	0	0	0	0	0	0	0	1	0	0	1			
		POINT ARENA	0	0	0	1	0	0	0	0	0	0	1	0	0	0	0	2			
		UKIAH	0	0	0	0	0	0	0	0	0	0	0	0	0	0	0	0			
		WILLITS	0	0	0	0	0	0	0	0	0	0	0	0	0	0	0	0			
	COUNTY TOTAL		0	0	0	1	1	0	0	0	0	0	1	0	1	1	0	5	0	1.00	60.0%
	REGION TOTAL		0	0	0	3	1	0	0	0	0	0	2	0	2	3	0	11	0		
NORTH EAST	LASSEN		0	0	0	0	1	0	0	1	0	0	0	1	1	1	0	5			
		SUSANVILLE	0	0	0	0	0	0	0	0	0	0	0	0	0	0	0	0			
	COUNTY TOTAL		0	0	0	0	1	0	0	1	0	0	0	1	1	1	0	5	0	2.50	50.0%
	MODOC		0	0	0	0	0	0	0	0	0	0	0	0	0	0	0	0			
	COUNTY TOTAL		0	0	0	0	0	0	0	0	0	0	0	0	0	0	0	0	0	0.00	0.0%
	NEVADA		0	0	0	1	0	0	0	0	0	0	1	0	0	0	0	2			
		GRASS VALLEY	0	0	0	1	0	0	0	0	0	0	0	0	1	0	0	2			
		NEVADA CITY	0	0	0	0	0	0	0	0	0	0	0	0	0	0	0	0			
	COUNTY TOTAL		0	0	0	2	0	0	0	0	0	0	1	0	1	0	0	4	0	1.33	66.7%
	PLUMAS		0	0	0	1	1	0	0	1	0	0	1	0	1	1	0	6			
		PORTOLA	0	0	0	0	0	0	0	0	0	0	0	0	1	1	0	2			
	COUNTY TOTAL		0	0	0	1	1	0	0	1	0	0	1	0	2	2	0	8	0	4.00	100.0%
	SIERRA		0	0	0	0	0	0	0	0	0		0	0	0	1	0	1			
	COUNTY TOTAL		0	0	0	0	0	0	0	0	0		0	0	0	1	0	1	0	1.00	100.0%
	REGION TOTAL		0	0	0	3	2	0	0	2	0	0	2	1	4	4	0	18	0		

GEOGRAPHICAL LOCATION	COUNTY	CITY	Q8F	Q9	Q10	Q11	Q12A	Q12B	Q12C	Q12D	Q17A	Q17B	Q18	Q19	Q20	Q25	Q26	TOTAL	Q26 PEND	AVG NO OF MEAS.	% W/ MEAS.
			|RESIDENTIAL, COMMERCIAL AND OTHER GROWTH CONTROL MEASURES|																			
SACRAMENTO	EL DORADO		0	0	0	0	0	0	0	0	0	0	0	0	0	0	0	0			
		PLACERVILLE	0	0	0	0	0	0	0	0	0	0	0			0	0	0			
		SOUTH LAKE T	0	0	1	1	1	0	0	0	1	1	1	1	1	0	0	8			
	COUNTY TOTAL		0	0	1	1	1	0	0	0	1	1	1	1	1	0	0	8	0	2.67	33.3%
	PLACER		0	0	1	0	0	0	0	0	1	1	0	1	1	0	0	5			
		AUBURN	0	0	0	0	1	0	0	0	0	0	0	0	0	0	0	1			
		COLFAX	0	0	0	0	1	0	0	0	0	0	0	1	0	0	0	2			
		LINCOLN	0	0	0	0	0	0	0	0	0	0	0	0	0	0	0	0			
		LOOMIS	0	0	0	0	0	0	0	0	0	0	0	0	0	0	0	0			
		ROCKLIN	0	0	0	1	0	0	0	0	0	0	1	0	1	0	0	3			
		ROSEVILLE	1	0	0	0	0	0	0	0	0	0	0	0	0	0	0	1			
	COUNTY TOTAL		1	0	1	1	2	0	0	0	1	1	1	2	2	0	0	12	0	1.71	71.4%
	SACRAMENTO		0	0	0	0	0	0	0	0	0	0	0	0	0	0	0	0			
		GALT	0	0	0	0	0	0	0	0	0	0	0	0	0	0	0	0			
		SACRAMENTO	0	0	0	0	0	0	0	0	0	0	0	0	0	0	0	0			
	COUNTY TOTAL		0	0	0	0	0	0	0	0	0	0	0	0	0	0	0	0	0	0.00	0.0%
	SAN JOAQUIN		1	0	0	1	0	0	0	0	0	0	1	0	0	0	0	3			
		ESCALON	0	1	1	1	0	0	0	0	0	0	0	0	1	0	0	4			
		LODI	1	0	0	1	0	0	0	1	0	0	1	1	0	1	0	6	1		
		MANTECA	1	1	1	1	0	0	0	0	0	0	1	0	0	1	0	6			
		RIPON	0	0	0	0	0	0	0	0	0	0	0	0	1	0	0	1			
		STOCKTON	0	0	0	0	0	0	0	0	0	0	0	0	0	0	0	0			
		TRACY	1	0	1	1	0	0	0	0	0	0	1	0	1	0	0	5			
	COUNTY TOTAL		4	2	3	5	0	0	0	1	0	0	4	1	3	2	0	25	1	3.57	85.7%

GEOGRAPHICAL LOCATION	COUNTY	CITY	RESIDENTIAL, COMMERCIAL AND OTHER GROWTH CONTROL MEASURES																TOTAL	Q26 PEND	AVG NO OF MEAS.	% W/ MEAS.
			Q8F	Q9	Q10	Q11	Q12A	Q12B	Q12C	Q12D	Q17A	Q17B	Q18	Q19	Q20	Q25	Q26				
	STANISLAUS		0	0	0	0	0	0	0	0	0	0	0	0	0	0	0	0			
		CERES	0	0	0	0	0	0	0	0	0	0	0	0	0	1	0	1			
		HUGHSON	0	0	0	1	0	0	0	0	0	0	0	0	1	0	0	2			
		MODESTO	1	0	0	0	0	0	0	0	0	0	0	0	0	1	1	3			
		OAKDALE	0	0	0	0	0	0	0	0	0	0	0	0	0	0	0	0			
		PATTERSON	1	0	0	0	0	0	0	0	0	0	0	0	0	0	0	1			
		RIVERBANK	0	0	0	0	0	0	0	0	0	0	0	0	0	0	0	0			
		TURLOCK	0	0	0	1	0	0	0	0	0	0	1	0	0	1	0	3			
		WATERFORD	0	0	0	0	0	0	0	0	0	0	0	0	0	0	0	0			
	COUNTY TOTAL		2	0	0	2	0	0	0	0	0	0	1	0	1	3	1	10	0	1.11	55.6%
	YOLO		0	0	0	0	0	0	0	0	0	0	0	0	0	0	0	0			
		DAVIS	0	1	0	0	0	0	0	0	0	0	0	0	0	1	1	3			
		WEST SACRAME	0	0	0	0	0	0	0	0	0	0	0	1	1	0		2			
		WINTERS	0	0	0	1	0	0	0	0	0	0	1	0	1	0	0	3	1		
		WOODLAND	0	0	0	1	0	0	0	0	0	0	1	0	0	1	0	3			
	COUNTY TOTAL		0	1	0	2	0	0	0	0	0	0	2	1	2	2	1	11	1	2.20	80.0%
	REGION TOTAL		7	3	5	11	3	0	0	1	2	2	9	5	9	7	2	66	2		
SF BAY AREA	ALAMEDA		0	0	0	1	0	0	0	0	0	0	0	0	0	1	0	2			
		ALBANY	0	0	0	0	1	0	0	0	0	0	0	0	1	0	0	2			
		BERKELEY	0	0	0	0	1	0	0	0	0	0	1	1	1	0	0	4			
		DUBLIN	0	0	0	0	0	0	0	0	0	0	0	0	0	0	0	0			
		EMERYVILLE	0	0	0	0	1	0	0	0	0		0	0	1	0	0	2			
		FREMONT	0	0	0	1	0	0	0	0	0	0	0	0	0	0	0	1			
		HAYWARD	0	0	0	0	1	0	0	0	0	0	0	0	1	0	0	2			
		LIVERMORE	0	1	0	0	0	0	0	0	0	0	0	0	0	0	0	1			
		NEWARK	0	0	0	0	0	0	0	0	0	0	0	0	1	0	0	1			
		OAKLAND	0	0	0	0	1	0	0	0	0	0	0	0	0	0	0	1	1		
		PIEDMONT	0		0	0	1	1	0	0	0	0	0	0	0	0	0	2			
		PLEASANTON	0	1	1	1	0	0	0	0	0	0	1	0	0	0	0	4			
		SAN LEANDRO	0	0	0	0	0	0	0	0	0	0	0	0	0	0	0	0			
		UNION CITY	0	0	1	0	1	0	0	0	0	0	0	1	0	0	0	3			
	COUNTY TOTAL		0	2	2	3	7	1	0	0	0	0	2	2	5	1	0	25	1	1.79	85.7%

GEOGRAPHICAL LOCATION	COUNTY	CITY	Q8F	Q9	Q10	Q11	Q12A	Q12B	Q12C	Q12D	Q17A	Q17B	Q18	Q19	Q20	Q25	Q26	TOTAL	Q26 PEND	AVG NO OF MEAS.	% W/ MEAS.
	CONTRA COSTA		1	0	0	0	0	0	0	0	0	0	0	0	0	0	0	1	1		
		ANTIOCH	1	0	0	0	0	0	0	0	0	0	0	0	0	1	0	2			
		BRENTWOOD	0	1	1	1	0	0	0	0	0	0	0	0	0	1	0	4			
		CLAYTON	1	0	0	0	0	0	0	0	0	0	0	0	1	0	0	2	1		
		CONCORD	0	0	0	1	0	0	0	0	0	0	1	0	1	0	0	3			
		DANVILLE	0	0	0	0	0	0	0	0	0	0	1	0	1	0	0	2			
		HERCULES	0	0	0	0	0	0	0	0	0	0	0	0	0	1	1	2			
		LAFAYETTE	0	0	0	0	0	0	0	0	0	0	0	0	0	0	0	0			
		MARTINEZ	0	0	0	1	0	0	0	0	0	0	1	0	0	0	0	2			
		MORAGA	0	0	0	0	0	0	0	1	0	0	0	0	0	0	0	1			
		ORINDA	0	0	0	0	0	0	0	0	0		0	0	1	0	0	1			
		PINOLE	0	0	0	0	0	0	0	0	0	0	0	0	0	1	0	1			
		PLEASANT HIL	0	1	0	0	0	1	0	0	0	0	0	1	1	0	0	4			
		RICHMOND	1	0	0	0	0	0	0	0	0	0	0	0	0	0	0	1			
		SAN PABLO	1	0	0	0	0	0	0	0	0		0	0	0	0	0	1	1		
		SAN RAMON	0	0	0	0	0	0	0	0	0	0	0	0	0	0	0	0			
		WALNUT CREEK	1	0	0	1	0	1	0	0	0	0	1	0	1	0	0	5	1		
	COUNTY TOTAL		6	2	1	4	0	2	0	1	0	0	4	1	6	4	1	32	4	1.88	88.2%
	MARIN		0	0	0	0	0	0	0	0	0	0	0	0	0	1	0	1			
		CORTE MADERA	0	0	0	0	0	0	0	0	0	0	0	0	0	0	0	0			
		FAIRFAX	0	0	0	0	0	0	0	1	0	0	0	0	0	0	0	1			
		LARKSPUR	0	0	0	1	0	0	0	0	0	0	1	0	1	0	1	4			
		NOVATO	0	1	1	0	0	0	0	0	1	1	0	0	0	0	0	4			
		SAN ANSELMO	0	0	0	0	0	0	0	0	0	0	0	0	0	0	0	0			
		SAN RAFAEL	0	0	0	1	1	0	0	0	1		0	0	1	0	1	5			
		SAUSALITO	0	0	0	0	0	0	0	0	0	0	1	0	0	0	1	2			
	COUNTY TOTAL		0	1	1	2	1	0	0	1	2	1	2	0	2	1	3	17	0	2.13	75.0%
	NAPA		0	1	1	0	0	0	0	0	0	0	1	1	0	0	0	4			
		CALISTOGA	0	0	0	1	0	0	0	0	0	0	1	0	1	0	0	3			
		NAPA	0	1	0	1	0	0	0	0	0	0	1	0	0	1	0	4			
		YOUNTVILLE	0	0	0	0	0	0	0	0	0	0	0	0	1	0	0	1			
	COUNTY TOTAL		0	2	1	2	0	0	0	0	0	0	3	1	2	1	0	12	0	3.00	100.0%

RESIDENTIAL, COMMERCIAL AND OTHER GROWTH CONTROL MEASURES

GEOGRAPHICAL LOCATION	COUNTY	CITY	RESIDENTIAL, COMMERCIAL AND OTHER GROWTH CONTROL MEASURES																		Q26	AVG %
			Q8F	Q9	Q10	Q11	Q12A	Q12B	Q12C	Q12D	Q17A	Q17B	Q18	Q19	Q20	Q25	Q26	TOTAL	PEND	NO OF W/ MEAS.MEAS.
SAN FRANCISC	SAN FRANCISC		0	0	0	1	1	0	0	0	1		1	1	1	0	1	7		
COUNTY TOTAL			0	0	0	1	1	0	0	0	1		1	1	1	0	1	7	0	7.00 100.0%
SAN MATEO			0	0	1	0	0	1	1	0	0	0	0	0	1	1	0	5		
		ATHERTON	0	0	0	0	0	0	0	0	0	0	0	0	0	0	0	0		
		BELMONT	0	1	1	0	0	0	0	0	0	0	0	0	1	0	0	3		
		BRISBANE	0	0	0	0	0	0	0	0	0	0	0	0	1	0	0	1		
		BURLINGAME	0	0	0	0	0	0	0	0	0	0	0	0	0	0	0	0		
		COLMA	0	0	1	0	0	0	0	0	0	0	0	0	0	0	0	1		
		DALY CITY	0	0	0	1	0	0	0	0	0	0	1	0	0	0	0	2		
		EAST PALO AL	0	0	0	0	0	0	0	0	0	0	0	0	0	0	0	0		
		HALF MOON BA	1	1	0	0	1	0	0	1	0	0	0	1	0	0	0	5	1	
		MILLBRAE	0	0	0	0	0	0	0	0	0		0	0	0	0	0	0		
		PACIFICA	0	0	1	0	1	1	0	0	0	0	0	0	0	0	0	3		
		PORTOLA VALL	0	0	0	0	1	0	0	0	0	0	0	0	0	0	0	1		
		REDWOOD CITY	0	0	0	0	0	0	0	0	0	0	0	0	0	0	0	0		
		SAN BRUNO	0	0	0	0	0	1	0	0	0	0	0	0	0	0	1	2		
		SAN CARLOS	0	0	0	0	1	0	0	0	0	0	0	0	1	0	0	2		
		SAN MATEO	0	0	0	0	1	0	0	0	0	0	0	1	1	0	0	3		
		SOUTH SAN FR	0	0	0	1	1	0	0	1	0	0	1	0	1	0	0	5		
		WOODSIDE	0	0	0	0	1	0	0	0	0	0	0	0	1	0	0	2		
COUNTY TOTAL			1	2	4	2	7	3	1	2	0	0	2	2	7	1	1	35	1	2.06 70.6%

GEOGRAPHICAL LOCATION	COUNTY	CITY	Q8F	Q9	Q10	Q11	Q12A	Q12B	Q12C	Q12D	Q17A	Q17B	Q18	Q19	Q20	Q25	Q26	TOTAL	Q26 PEND	AVG NO OF MEAS.	% W/ MEAS.
	SANTA CLARA		0	0	0	0	1	0	0	1	0	0	0	0	0	1	0	3			
		CAMPBELL	0	0	0	0	0	0	0	0	0	0	0	0	1	0	0	1			
		CUPERTINO	0	0	0	1	0	0	0	0	1	1	1	0	1	1	0	6			
		GILROY	0	1	1	0	1	0	0	0	0	1	0	0	0	0	0	4			
		LOS ALTOS	0	0	0	0	0	0	0	0	0	0	0	0	0	0	0	0			
		LOS ALTOS HI	0	0	0	0	0	0	0	0	0	0	0	0	0	0	0	0	1		
		LOS GATOS	0	0	0	1	0	0	0	0	0	0	1	0	0	0	0	2			
		MILPITAS	0	0	0	1	0	0	0	1	0	0	1	1	0	0	1	5			
		MONTE SERENO	0	0	0	0	0	0	0	0	0	0	0	0	0	0	0	0			
		MORGAN HILL	0	1	1	0	0	0	0	0	0	0	0	0	0	0	0	2			
		MOUNTAIN VIE	0	0	0	0	0	0	0	0	0	0	0	1	0	0	0	1			
		PALO ALTO	0	0	0	0	1	0	0	0	1	1	1	1	1	0	0	6	1		
		SAN JOSE	1	0	0	1	1	0	0	1	0	1	1	1	1	1	0	9			
		SANTA CLARA	0	0	0	0	1	1	1	1	0	0	0	0	0	0	0	4			
		SARATOGA	0	0	0	1	1	0	0	0	0	0	0	0	0	0	0	2			
		SUNNYVALE	0	0	0	0	0	0	0	0	1	1	0	1	0	0	0	3			
	COUNTY TOTAL		1	2	2	5	6	1	1	4	3	5	5	5	4	3	1	48	2	3.00	81.3%
	SANTA CRUZ		1	1	1	0	0	0	0	0	0	0	0	0	1	1	0	5			
		CAPITOLA	0	0	0	0	0	0	0	0	0	0	0	0	0	0	0	0			
		SANTA CRUZ	1	1	1	0	0	0	0	1	0	0	0	0	0	1	0	5			
		SCOTTS VALLE	0	0	0	0	0	0	0	0	0	0	0	0	1	0	0	1			
		WATSONVILLE	0	0	0	0	0	0	0	0	0	0	0	1	1	0	0	2			
	COUNTY TOTAL		2	2	2	0	0	0	0	1	0	0	0	1	3	2	0	13	0	2.60	80.0%
	SOLANO		0	0	0	0	0	1	0	0	0	0	0	0	0	1	0	2			
		BENICIA	0	0	0	0	0	0	0	0	0	0	0	0	0	0	1	1			
		DIXON	0	1	1	1	1	0	0	0	0	0	1	0	0	0	0	5			
		FAIRFIELD	0	0	0	0	0	0	0	0	0	0	0	0	1	0	0	1			
		SUISUN CITY	0	0	0	0	0	0	0	0	0	0	0	0	0	0	0	0			
		VACAVILLE	0	0	0	1	1	0	0	0	0	0	1	0	1	0	0	4	1		
		VALLEJO	0	0	0	0	0	0	0	0	0	0	0	0	0	0	0	0			
	COUNTY TOTAL		0	1	1	2	2	1	0	0	0	0	2	0	1	2	1	13	1	1.86	71.4%

RESIDENTIAL, COMMERCIAL AND OTHER GROWTH CONTROL MEASURES

GEOGRAPHICAL LOCATION	COUNTY	CITY	RESIDENTIAL, COMMERCIAL AND OTHER GROWTH CONTROL MEASURES															TOTAL	Q26 PEND	AVG NO OF MEAS.	% W/MEAS.
			Q8F	Q9	Q10	Q11	Q12A	Q12B	Q12C	Q12D	Q17A	Q17B	Q18	Q19	Q20	Q25	Q26				
	SONOMA		0	0	0	0	0	0	0	0	0	0	0	1	0	0	0	1			
		CLOVERDALE	0	0	0	0	0	0	0	0	0	0	0	0	0	1	0	1	1		
		COTATI	0	0	1	0	1	0	0	0	0	0	0	0	0	1	0	3			
		HEALDSBURG	0	0	0	0	1	0	0	0	0	0	0	1	0	1	0	3			
		PETALUMA	0	0	0	0	0	0	0	0	0	0	0	0	0	1	1	2			
		ROHNERT PARK	0	0	1	0	0	0	0	0	0	0	0	0	0	0	0	1			
		SANTA ROSA	1	0	0	1	0	0	0	0	0	0	1	0	0	1	0	4			
		SEBASTOPOL	0	0	0	0	0	0	0	0	0	0	0	0	0	0	1	1			
		SONOMA	0	1	1	0	0	0	0	0	0	0	0	0	0	1	1	4			
	COUNTY TOTAL		1	1	3	1	2	0	0	0	0	0	1	2	0	6	3	20	1	2.22	100.0%
	REGION TOTAL		11	15	17	22	26	8	2	9	6	6	22	15	31	21	11	222	10		
SOUTH COAST	LOS ANGELES		0	0	0	1	1	0	0	1	0	0	1	0	1	0	0	5			
		AGOURA HILLS	0	0	0	1	0	0	0	1	0	0	1	1	1	0	0	5			
		ALHAMBRA	0	0	0	0	1	0	0	0	0	0	0	0	1	0	0	2	1		
		ARCADIA	0	0	0	0	0	0	0	0	0	0	0	0	0	0	0	0			
		ARTESIA	0	0	0	1	0	0	0	0	0	0	1	0	0	0	0	2	1		
		AVALON	0	1	1	0	0	0	0	0	1	1	0	0	1		0	5	1		
		AZUSA	0	0	0	0	0	0	0	0	0	0	0	0	0	0	1	1			
		BALDWIN PARK	0	0	0	0	1	0	0	0	0	0	0	0	0	0	0	1			
		BELL	0	0	0	0	1	0	0	0	0	0	0	0	0	0	0	1			
		BELL GARDENS	0	0	0	0	0	0	0	0	0	0	0	0	0	0	0	0			
		BELLFLOWER	0	0	0	0	1	0	0	0	0	0	0	0	0	0	0	1			
		BRADBURY	0	0	0	0	0	0	0	0	0	0	0	0	0	0	0	0			
		BURBANK	0	0	0	0	0	0	0	0	0	0	0	0	1	0	0	1	1		
		CLAREMONT	0	0	0	0	0	0	0	0	0	0	0	0	0	0	0	0			
		COMMERCE	0	0	0	0	0	0	0	0	0	0	0	0	0	0	0	0			
		COVINA	0	0	0	0	0	0	0	0	0	0	0	1	0	0	0	1	1		
		CUDAHY	0	0	0	0	1	0	0	0	0	0	0	0	1	0	0	2			
		CULVER CITY	1	0	0	1	1	0	0	0	0	0	1	0	1	0	0	5	1		
		DOWNEY	0	0	0	1	0	0	0	0	0	0	1	0	1	0	0	3			
		DUARTE	0	0	0	1	0	0	0	0	0	0	1	0	0	0	0	2			
		EL SEGUNDO	0	0	0	0	0	0	0	0	0	0	0	1	0	0	0	1			
		GARDENA	0	0	0	1	1	0	0	0	0	0	1	0	0	0	0	3			
		GLENDALE	0	0	0	0	1	0	0	0	0	0	0	0	1	0	0	2			
		GLENDORA	0	0	0	0	0	0	0	0	0	0	0	0	0	0	0	0			
		HAWAIIAN GAR	0	0	0	0	0	0	0	0	0	0	0	0	0	0	0	0			
		HAWTHORNE	0	0	0	0	0	0	0	0	0	0	0	0	0	0	0	0			
		HERMOSA BEAC	0	0	0	1	1	1	0	0	0	0	1	1	1	0	0	6			
		HIDDEN HILLS	0	0	0	1	0	0	0	0	0	0	0	0	1	0	0	2			
		HUNTINGTON P	0	0	0	0	0	0	0	0	0	0	0	0	0	0	0	0			
		INGLEWOOD	0	0	0	0	1	0	0	0	0	0	0	0	0	0	0	1			
		IRWINDALE	0	0	0	0	0	0	0	0	0	0	0	0	0	0	0	0			

GEOGRAPHICAL LOCATION	COUNTY	CITY	Q8F	Q9	Q10	Q11	Q12A	Q12B	Q12C	Q12D	Q17A	Q17B	Q18	Q19	Q20	Q25	Q26	TOTAL	Q26 PEND	AVG NO OF MEAS.	% W/ MEAS.
		LA CANADA FL	0	0	0	0	1	0	0	0					0	0		1			
		LA HABRA HEI	0	0	0	0	0	0	0	0	0	0	0	0	1	0	0	1			
		LA MIRADA	0	0	0	0	0	0	0	0	0	0	0	0	0	0	0	0			
		LA PUENTE	0	0	0	0	1	0	0	0	0	0	0	0	0	0	0	1			
		LA VERNE	0	0	0	1	0	0	0	0	0	0	0	0	0	0	0	1	1		
		LAKEWOOD	0	0	0	1	1	0	0	0	0	0	1	0	0	0	0	3			
		LANCASTER	0	0	0	0	0	0	0	0	0	0	0	0	1	0	0	1			
		LAWNDALE	0	0	0	0	0	0	0	0	0	0	0	0	0	0	0	0			
		LOMITA	0	0	0	0	0	0	0	0	0		0	0	0	0	0	0			
		LONG BEACH	0	0	0	0	1	0	0	0	0	0	0	0	0	0	0	1			
		LOS ANGELES	1	0	1	1	1	0	0	0	1	0	1	1		0	1	8			
		LYNWOOD	0	0	0	1	0	0	0	0	0	0	1	0	0	0	0	2			
		MANHATTAN BE	0	0	0	0	0	0	0	0	0	0	0	0	0	0	0	0			
		MAYWOOD	0	1	0	1	1	0	1	0	0	0	1	0	0	0	0	5			
		MONROVIA	0	0	0	0	1	0	0	0	0	0	0	0	0	0	0	1			
		MONTEBELLO	0	0	0	0	1	0	0	0	0	0	0	0	1	0	0	2	1		
		MONTEREY PAR	0	1	1	1	1	1	0	0	0	0	0	1	1	0	0	7			
		NORWALK	0	0	0	0	1	0	0	0	0	0	0	0	0	0	0	1			
		PALOS VERDES	0	0	0	1	0	0	0	0	0	0	0	0	1	1	0	3			
		PARAMOUNT	0	0	0	0	1	0	0	0	0	0	0	0	0	0	0	1			
		PASADENA	1		1	0	1	0	0	0	1	1	1	0	1	0	1	8			
		PICO RIVERA	0	0	0	0	1	0	0	0	0	0	0	0	0	0	0	1			
		POMONA	0	0	0	0	0	0	0	0	0	0	0	0	0	0	0	0	1		
		RANCHO PALOS	0	0	0	0	0	0	0	0	0	0	0	0	0	0	0	0	1		
		REDONDO BEAC	1	0	0	0	1	0	0	0	0	0	0	0	0	0	0	2			
		ROLLING HILL	0	0	0	0	0	0	0	0	0	0	0	0	1	0	0	1			
		ROSEMEAD	0	0	0	0	1	0	0	0	0	0	0	0	1	0	0	2			
		SAN DIMAS	0	0	0	0	0	0	0	0	0	0	0	0	0	0	0	0			
		SAN FERNANDO	0	0	0	0	0	0	0	0	0	0	0	0	0	0	0	0			
		SAN GABRIEL	0	0	0	0	1	0	0	0	0	0	0	0	1	0	0	2			
		SAN MARINO	0	0	0	0	0	0	0	0	0	0	0	0	0	0	1	1			
		SANTA CLARIT	0	0	0	0	0	0	0	0	0	0	0	0	0	0	0	0			
		SANTA MONICA	0	0	0	0	1	0	0	0	0	0	0	0	1	0	0	2	1		
		SIGNAL HILL	0	0	0	0	1	0	0	0	0	0	0	1	0	0	0	2			
		SOUTH EL MON	0	0	0	0	1	0	0	0	0	0	0	0	0	0	0	1			
		SOUTH GATE	0	0	0	0	1	0	0	0	0	0	0	0	0	0	0	1			
		TORRANCE	0	0	0	1	0	0	0	0	0	0	1	1	0	0	0	3			
		VERNON	0	0	0	0	0	0	0	0	0	1	0	0	0	0	0	1			
		WALNUT	0	0	0	0	0	0	0	0	0	0	0	0	0	0	0	0			
		WEST COVINA	0	0	0	0	0	0	0	0	0	0	0	0	0	0	0	0			
		WEST HOLLYWO	0	0	0	1	1	0	0	0	0	0	1	0	1	0	0	4	1		
		WHITTIER	0	0	0	0	1	1	0	0	0	0	0	0	0	0	0	2			
COUNTY TOTAL			4	3	4	18	33	3	1	2	3	3	15	7	23	1	4	124	12	1.70	71.2%

GEOGRAPHICAL LOCATION	COUNTY	CITY	RESIDENTIAL, COMMERCIAL AND OTHER GROWTH CONTROL MEASURES															TOTAL	Q26 PEND	AVG NO OF MEAS.	% W/ MEAS.
			Q8F	Q9	Q10	Q11	Q12A	Q12B	Q12C	Q12D	Q17A	Q17B	Q18	Q19	Q20	Q25	Q26				
	ORANGE		1	0	0	0	0	0	0	0	0	0	0	0	0	0	0	1			
		ANAHEIM	0	0	0	0	0	0	0	0	0	0	0	0	0	0	0	0			
		BREA	0	0	0	0	0	0	0	0	0	0	0	0	0	0	0	0			
		BUENA PARK	0	0	0	0	0	0	0	0	0	0	0	0	0	0	0	0			
		COSTA MESA	0	0	0	1	0	0	0	0	0	0	1	0	0	0	0	2			
		CYPRESS	0	0	0	0	0	0	0	0	0	0	0	1	1	0	1	3			
		FOUNTAIN VAL	0	0	0	1	0	0	0	0	0	0	1	0	0	0	0	2			
		GARDEN GROVE	1	0	0	0	0	0	0	0	0	0	0	0	0	0	1	2			
		HUNTINGTON B	0	0	0	1	0	0	0	0	0	0	0	0	0	1	0	2	1		
		IRVINE	0	0	0	0	0	0	0	1	0	0	0	0	0	0	0	1	1		
		LA HABRA	0	0	0	0	0	0	0	0	0	0	0	0	0	0	0	0	1		
		LA PALMA	1	0	0	1	0	0	1	0			1	0	0	0	0	4			
		LAGUNA BEACH	0	0	0	0	0	0	0	0	0	0	0	0	0	0	0	0			
		LOS ALAMITOS	1	0	0	0	0	0	0	0	0	0	0	0	0	0	0	1			
		MISSION VIEJ	1	0	0	0	0	0	0	0	0	0	0	0	0	0	0	1			
		NEWPORT BEAC	0	0	0	1	1	0	0	0	0	0	1	1	0	0	0	4			
		ORANGE	0	0	0	0	0	0	0	0	0	0	0	0	0	0	0	0			
		PLACENTIA	0	0	0	0	0	0	0	0	0		0	0	0	0	0	0			
		SAN CLEMENTE	1	1	1	0	0	0	0	0	0	0	0	0	0	0	0	3	1		
		SAN JUAN CAP	0	1	1	1	0	0	0	0	0	0	1	0	1	1	0	6			
		SANTA ANA	0	0	0	0	1	0	0	0	0	0	0	0	0	0	0	1			
		SEAL BEACH	0	0	0	0	1	0	0	0	0	0	0	0	0	0	0	1			
		STANTON	0	0	0	0	1	0	0	0	0	0	0	0	0	0	0	1			
		TUSTIN	0	0	0	0	0	0	0	0	0	0	0	0	0	0	0	0			
		VILLA PARK	0	0	0	0	1	0	0	0	0	0	0	0	0	0	0	1			
		WESTMINSTER	0	0	0	0	0	0	0	0	0	0	0		0	0	0	0			
		YORBA LINDA	0	0	0	0	0	0	0	0	0		0	0	0	0	0	0			
	COUNTY TOTAL		6	2	2	6	5	0	1	1	0	0	5	2	2	2	2	36	4	1.33	63.0%

GEOGRAPHICAL LOCATION	COUNTY	CITY	RESIDENTIAL, COMMERCIAL AND OTHER GROWTH CONTROL MEASURES															TOTAL	Q26 PEND	AVG NO OF MEAS.	% W/ MEAS.
			Q8F	Q9	Q10	Q11	Q12A	Q12B	Q12C	Q12D	Q17A	Q17B	Q18	Q19	Q20	Q25	Q26				
	SAN DIEGO		0	0	0	0	0	0	0	0	0	0	0	0	0	1	0	1	1		
		CARLSBAD	1	0	0	1	1	0	0	0	0	0	1	0	1	0	0	5			
		CHULA VISTA	1	0	0	1	1	1	1	0	0	0	1	0	0	1	0	7	1		
		CORONADO	0	0	0	0	1	0	0	0	0	0	0	0	0	0	0	1			
		DEL MAR	0	0	0	0	0	0	0	0	1		1	1	0	0	1	4			
		ENCINITAS	1	0	0	1	1	0	0	1	0	0	1	1	1	0	0	7	1		
		ESCONDIDO	1	1	1	1	1	0	1	0	0	0	1	0	0	0	0	7	1		
		IMPERIAL BEA	0	0	0	0	1	0	0	0	0	0	0	0	0	0	0	1			
		LA MESA	0	0	0	0	0	0	0	0	0	0	0	0	0	0	0	0			
		LEMON GROVE	0	0	0	0	0	0	0	0	0	0	0	0	0	0	0	0			
		NATIONAL CIT	0	0	0	0	1	0	0	0	0	0	0	1	0	0	1	3			
		OCEANSIDE	1	1	1	1	1	0	0	0	0	0	0	0	0	0	0	5	1		
		POWAY	0	0	0	0	0	1	0	0	0	0	0	0	0	0	0	1			
		SAN DIEGO	1	0	1	0	0	0	0	0	0	0	0	0	0	1	1	4			
		SAN MARCOS	1	0	0	1	1	0	0	1	0	0	1	0	1	0	0	6			
		SANTEE	0	0	0	0	1	0	0	0	0	0	0	0	1	0	0	2			
		SOLANA BEACH	0	0	0	0	0	1	1	0	0	0	1	0	0	0	1	4			
		VISTA	0	1	1	1	0	1	0	0	0	0	0	0	0	0	0	4			
	COUNTY TOTAL		7	3	4	7	10	4	3	2	1	0	7	3	4	3	4	62	5	3.44	88.9%
	VENTURA		0	0	1	1	1	0	0	1	0	0	1	1	0	1	0	7			
		CAMARILLO	0	1	1	0	0	0	0	0	0	0	0	1	1	0	0	4			
		FILLMORE	0	1	1	0	0	0	0	0	0	0	0	0	0	1	0	3	1		
		OJAI	0	1	1	1	0	0	0	0	0	0	0	0	0	0	0	3	1		
		OXNARD	1	0	0	1	0	0	0	0	0	0	1	0	0	1	1	5			
		PORT HUENEME	0	0	0	0	0	0	0	1	0	0	0	1	1	0	0	3			
		SANTA PAULA	0	1	1	0	0	0	0	0	0	0	0	0	0	1	0	3			
		SIMI VALLEY	0	1	1	1	0	0	0	0	0	0	0	0	0	1	0	4			
		THOUSAND OAK	0	0	1	0	0	0	0	0	0	0	0	0	0	0	0	1			
		VENTURA	1	1	1	1	1	0	0	0	0	0	0	0	0	1	1	7			
	COUNTY TOTAL		2	6	8	5	2	0	0	2	0	0	2	3	2	6	2	40	2	4.00	100.0%
	REGION TOTAL		19	14	18	36	50	7	5	7	4	3	29	15	31	12	12	262	23		

GEOGRAPHICAL LOCATION	COUNTY	CITY	Q8F	Q9	Q10	Q11	Q12A	Q12B	Q12C	Q12D	Q17A	Q17B	Q18	Q19	Q20	Q25	Q26	TOTAL	Q26 PEND	AVG NO OF MEAS.	% W/ MEAS.
SOUTH INLAND	IMPERIAL		0	0	0	0	0	0	0	0	0	0	0	0	0	0	0	0			
		EL CENTRO	1	0	0	0	0	0	0	0	0	0	0	0	0	1	0	2			
		HOLTVILLE	0	0	0	0	0	0	0	0	0	0	0	0	0	0	0	0			
		IMPERIAL	0	0	0	1	0	0	0	0	1	1	1	1	0	0	0	5			
	COUNTY TOTAL		1	0	0	1	0	0	0	0	1	1	1	1	0	1	0	7	0	1.75	50.0%
	RIVERSIDE		1	0	0	0	0	0	0	0	0	0	0	0	0	0	0	1			
		BANNING	0	0	0	0	0	0	0	0	0	0	0	0	0	0	0	0	1		
		BEAUMONT	0	0	0	0	1	0	0	0	0	0	0	0	0	0	0	1			
		BLYTHE	0	0	0	1	0	0	0	0	0	0	1	0	1	0	0	3			
		CATHEDRAL CI	0	0	0	0	0	0	0	0	0	0	0	0	0	0	0	0	1		
		CORONA	0	0	1	1	1	0	0	0	0	0	1	0	0	0	1	5			
		HEMET	0	1	0	1	0	1	0	0	0	0	0	0	0	0	0	3	1		
		INDIO	0	0	0	0	0	0	0	0	0		0	0	0	0	0	0			
		LA QUINTA	0	0	0	0	0	0	0	0	0	0	0	0	0	0	0	0			
		MORENO VALLE	0	0	0	1	0	0	0	0	0	0	1	0	0	0	0	2	1		
		NORCO	0	1	0	1	1	0	0	0	0	0	1	0	0	0	0	4			
		PALM DESERT	0	0	0	0	0	0	0	0	0	0	0	0	0	0	0	0			
		PALM SPRINGS	0	0	0	0	0	0	0	0	0	0	0	0	0	0	0	0			
		PERRIS	0	0	0	0	0	0	0	0	0	0	1	0	1	0	0	2	1		
		RANCHO MIRAG	0	0	0	1	1	0	0	1	0	0	0	0	0	0	0	3			
		RIVERSIDE	1	0	1	0	1	1	0	1	0	0	0	1	0	0	0	6			
		SAN JACINTO	0	0	0	0	1	0	0	0	0	0	0	0	0	0	0	1			
	COUNTY TOTAL		2	2	2	6	6	2	0	2	0	0	5	1	2	0	1	31	5	1.82	64.7%

The column grouping header reads: RESIDENTIAL, COMMERCIAL AND OTHER GROWTH CONTROL MEASURES

GEOGRAPHICAL LOCATION	COUNTY	CITY	RESIDENTIAL, COMMERCIAL AND OTHER GROWTH CONTROL MEASURES															TOTAL	Q26 PEND	AVG NO OF MEAS.	% W/ MEAS.
			Q8F	Q9	Q10	Q11	Q12A	Q12B	Q12C	Q12D	Q17A	Q17B	Q18	Q19	Q20	Q25	Q26				
	SAN BERNARDI		1	0	0	0	0	0	0	0	0		0	0	0	0	0	1	1		
		ADELANTO	0	0	0	1	1	0	0	0	0	0	0	0	1	0	0	3			
		BARSTOW	0	0	0	0	0	0	0	0	0	0	0	0	0	0	0	0			
		CHINO	0	0	0	0	1	1	0	0	0	0	0	0	0	0	0	2			
		COLTON	0	0	0	0	1	0	0	0	0	0	0	0	0	0	0	1			
		FONTANA	0	0	0	0	0	0	0	0	0	0	0	0	0	0	0	0	1		
		GRAND TERRAC	0	0	0	0	0	0	0	0	0	0	0	0	0	0	0	0			
		HESPERIA	0	0	0	0	0	0	0	0	0	0	0	0	1	0	0	1			
		HIGHLAND	0	0	0		0	0	0	0	0	0	0	0	0	0	0	0			
		MONTCLAIR	0	0	0	1	0	0	0	0	0	0	0	0	0	0	0	1			
		NEEDLES	0	0	0	0	0	0	0	0	0	0	0	0	0	0	0	0			
		ONTARIO	0	0	0	1	0	0	0	0	0	0	0	0	1	0	0	2			
		RANCHO CUCAM	0	0	0	1	0	0	0	0	0	0	1	0	0	0	0	2			
		REDLANDS	1	1	1	1	0	0	0	0	0	0	0	0	0	0	0	4			
		RIALTO	0	0	0	0	1	0	0	0	0	0	0	1	0	0	0	2			
		SAN BERNARDI	0	0	0	0	1	0	0	0	0	0	0	1	1	0	1	4			
		TWENTYNINE P	0	0	0	0	1	0	0	0	0	0	0	1	1	0	0	3			
		UPLAND	0	0	0	1	0	0	0	0	0	0	1	0	0	0	0	2			
		VICTORVILLE	0	0	0	0	1	0	0	0	0	0	0	0	0	0	0	1			
	COUNTY TOTAL		2	1	1	6	7	1	0	0	0	0	2	3	5	0	1	29	2	1.53	73.7%
	REGION TOTAL		5	3	3	13	13	3	0	2	1	1	8	5	7	1	2	67	7		

Appendix D
MAP DISTRIBUTION OF ALL MEASURES: LOCATION OF JURISDICTIONS WITH MEASURES

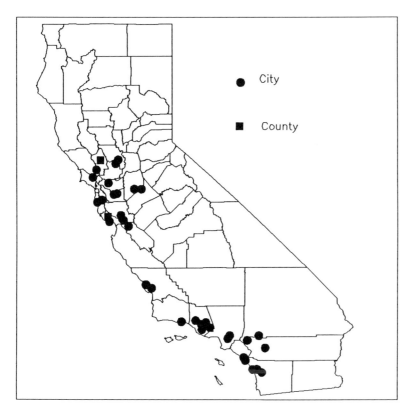

Figure D–1. Jurisdictions with Population Growth Limitations

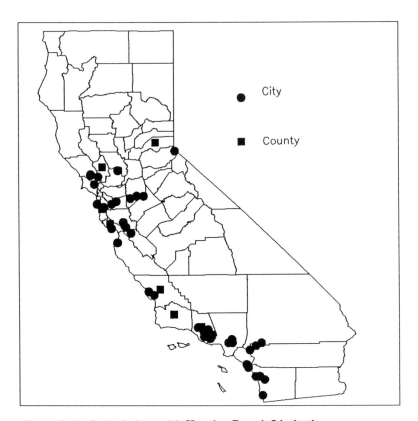

Figure D–2. Jurisdictions with Housing Permit Limitations

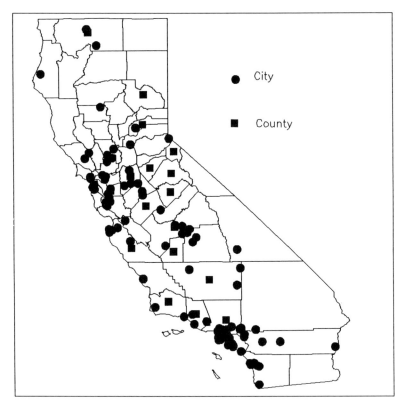

Figure D–3. Jurisdictions with Residential Infrastructure Requirements

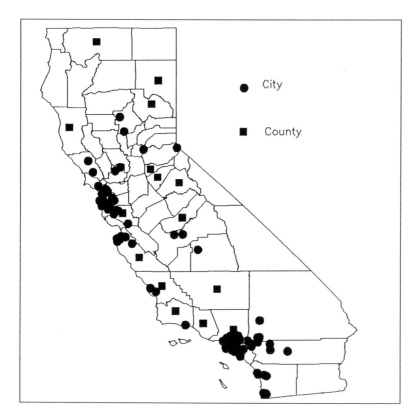

Figure D–4. Jurisdictions That Have Reduced the Permitted Residential Density by General Plan or Rezoning

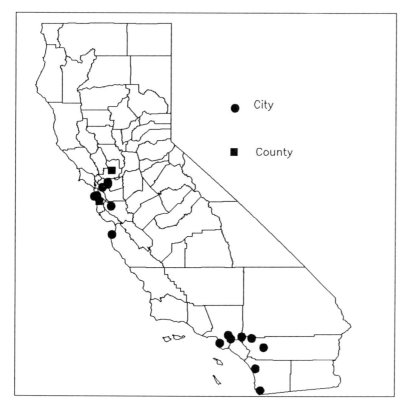

Figure D–5. Jurisdictions Where Voter Approval is Required for Density Increases

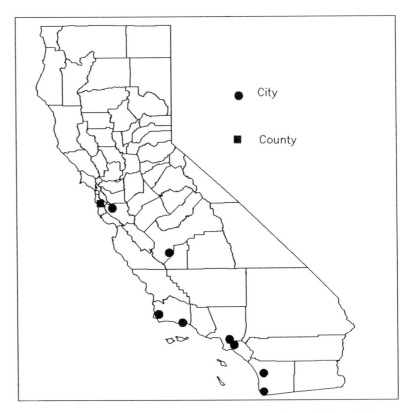

Figure D–6. Jurisdictions Where a Supermajority Council/Board Vote is Required for Density Increases

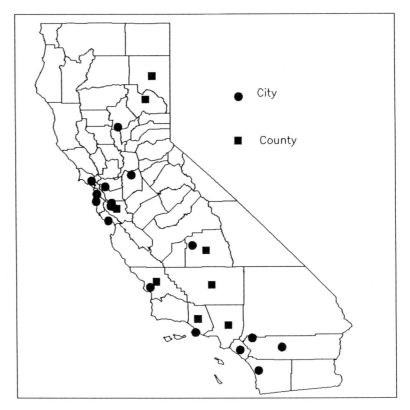

Figure D–7. Jurisdictions That Have Rezoned Residential Land to Agricultural or Open Space

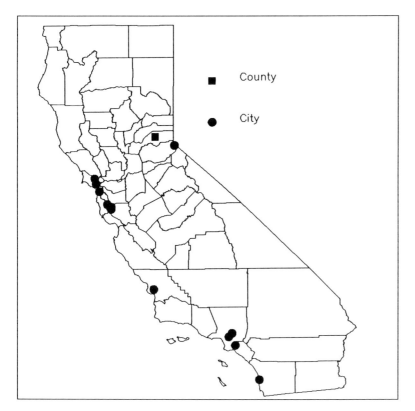

Figure D–8. Jurisdictions with Commercial Square Footage Limitations

Figure D–9. Jurisdictions with Industrial Square Footage Limitations

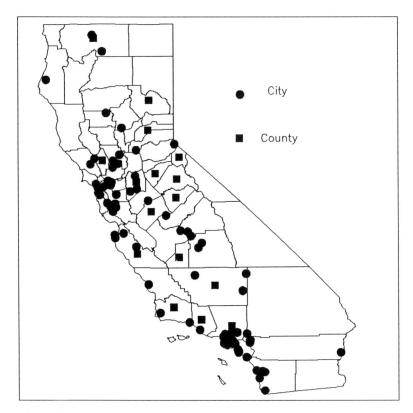

**Figure D–10. Jurisdictions with Commercial or Industrial
Infrastructure Requirements**

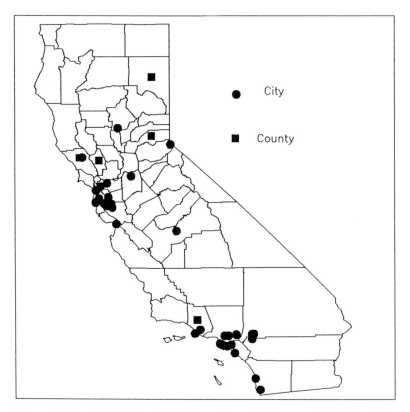

**Figure D–11. Jurisdictions That Have Rezoned Commercial/Industrial
Land to Less Intense Uses**

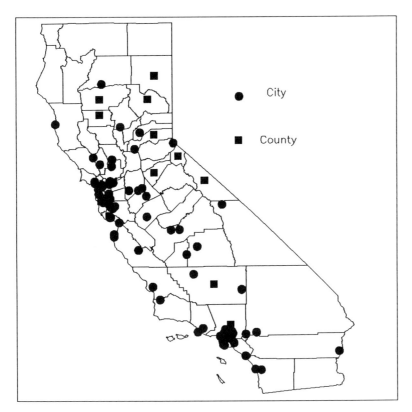

Figure D–12. Jurisdictions That Have Restricted Commercial Building Height in the Last Five Years

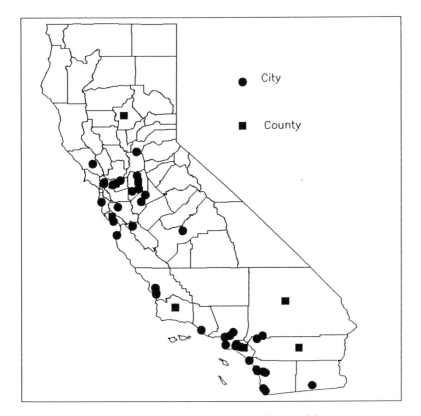

Figure D–13. Jurisdictions with General Plan Growth Management Elements Adopted or Pending

Figure D–14. Jurisdictions That Have Established an Urban Limit Line or Greenbelt

Figure D–15. Jurisdictions That Have Enacted "Other" Measures

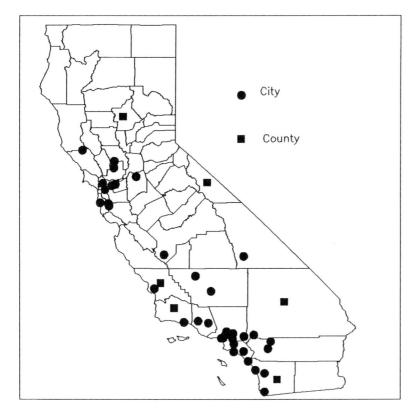

Figure D–16. Jurisdictions That Have Growth Measures Pending as of December 1988

Appendix E

GROWTH MEASURE MODELS FOR SELECTED COUNTIES: LOS ANGELES AND SAN FRANCISCO BAY METROPOLITAN AREAS

Table E-1. Stage 1—Enactment Models: Relationship between Hypothesized Variables and Annual Number of Growth Control Measures in Selected Counties, 1970–1988 (n=19)

I. Los Angeles County

Variable	Regression coefficient (Standard error) [t]p				
	Los Angeles (R^2=0.82)	Orange (R^2=0.74)	Ventura (R^2=0.45)	Riverside (R^2=0.79)	San Bernardino (R^2=0.58)
Intercept	1.40	8.40	– 12.34	2.57	1.64
Population of county (no lag)	0.00000315 (0.00000069) [4.57]***	0.00000343 (0.00000107) [3.20]**	0.00001763 (0.00000641) [2.75]*	– 0.00000049 (0.00000274) [– 0.18]	0.00000658 (0.00000215) [3.06]**
Value of non-residential construction (3-year lag)	– 0.00001608 (0.00000609) [– 2.64]*	– 0.00002767 (0.00000571) [– 4.84]***	0.00006946 (0.00004066) [1.71]	– 0.00001748 (0.00000700) [– 2.50]*	0.00003538 (0.00001519) [– 2.33]*
Square of the value of non-residential construction (3-year lag)	2.676×10^{-12} (9.477×10^{-13}) [2.82]*	1.291×10^{-11} (1.536×10^{-12}) [5.09]***	$- 2.129 \times 10^{-10}$ (1.143×10^{-10}) [– 1.86]	3.488×10^{-11} (8.052×10^{-12}) [4.33]***	4.099×10^{-11} (2.026×10^{-11}) [2.02]
Durbin-Watson d	2.24 ns	1.39 inc.	1.69 ns	2.28 ns	2.26 ns

Notes:
* $p < 0.05$.
** $p < 0.01$.
*** $p < 0.001$.
ns   p not significant.
inc.   d is inconclusive.

Table E-1 (continued)

II. San Francisco Bay Area

Variable	Regression coefficient (Standard error) [t]^p				
	San Francisco (R^2=0.28)	Alameda (R^2=0.47)	San Mateo (R^2=0.46)	Santa Clara (R^2=0.22)	Marin (R^2=0.32)
Intercept	− 9.52	− 19.99	− 26.03	− 3.40	− 14.04
Population of county (no lag)	0.00001381 (0.00000871) [1.59]	0.00001781 (0.00000756) [2.36]*	0.00005265 (0.00001841) [2.86]*	0.00000624 (0.00000438) [1.43]	0.00007333 (0.00004954) [1.48]
Value of non-residential construction (3-year lag)	− 0.00000051 (0.00000248) [− 0.21]	0.00000185 (0.00001317) [0.14]	− 0.00002414 (0.00004345) [− 0.56]	− 0.00000675 (0.00001053) [− 0.64]	− 0.00006314 (0.00010657) [− 0.59]
Square of the value of non-residential construction (3-year lag)	8.363×10^{-13} (1.590×10^{-12}) [0.53]	$- 9.129 \times 10^{-13}$ (1.303×10^{-11}) [− 0.07]	3.817×10^{-11} (8.383×10^{-11}) [0.46]	3.522×10^{-12} (5.465×10^{-12}) [0.64]	6.0×10^{-10} (7.0×10^{-10}) [0.78]
Durbin-Watson d	1.34 inc.	1.43 inc.	2.02 ns	2.48 ns	1.12 inc.

Variable	Contra Costa (R^2=0.50)	Solano (R^2=0.21)	Napa (R^2=0.27)	Santa Cruz (R^2=0.05)	Sonoma (R^2=0.51)
Intercept	− 4.74	− 1.36	− 4.46	− 1.37	− 3.42
Population of county (no lag)	0.00000345 (0.00000900) [0.38]	0.00001005 (0.00000515) [1.95]	0.00004802 (0.00003126) [1.54]	0.00000579 (0.00000864) [0.67]	0.00001840 (0.00000510) [3.61]**
Value of non-residential construction (3-year lag)	0.00001835 (0.00001777) [1.03]	− 0.00001061 (0.00001954) [− 0.54]	0.00003787 (0.00007714) [0.49]	0.00003993 (0.00009347) [0.43]	− 0.00000699 (0.00002568) [− 0.27]
Square of the value of non-residential construction (3-year lag)	$- 1.598 \times 10^{-11}$ (2.293×10^{-12}) [− 0.70]	2.491×10^{-11} (4.969×10^{-11}) [0.50]	$- 6.628 \times 10^{-10}$ (7.879×10^{-10}) [− 0.84]	$- 4.573 \times 10^{-10}$ (8.969×10^{-10}) [− 0.51]	$- 1.493 \times 10^{-11}$ (8.781×10^{-11}) [− 0.17]
Durbin-Watson d	1.43 inc.	2.04 ns	1.95 ns	1.48 inc.	2.29 ns

Table E-2. Stage 2—Effects Models: Relationship between Hypothesized Variables and Permit Value of Construction in Selected Regions, 1973–1988 (n=16)

Model 1: Permit value of non-residential construction, in thousands of dollars
Model 2: Permit value of residential construction, in thousands of dollars

I. Los Angeles Metropolitan Area

	Regression coefficient (Standard error) $[t]^p$					
Variable	Los Angeles		Orange		Ventura	
	Model 1 (R^2=0.77)	Model 2 (R^2=0.93)	Model 1 (R^2=0.79)	Model 2 (R^2=0.73)	Model 1 (R^2=0.66)	Model 2 (R^2=0.60)
Intercept	– $7,175,065	– $14,903,913	– $1,266,003	$1,172,869	– $94,877	– $437,921
Population (no lag)	$1.384 (0.36) [3.89]**	$2.672 (0.32) [8.36]***	$1.546 (0.35) [4.37]***	$0.976 (0.769) [1.27]	$0.554 (0.16) [3.46]**	$0.665 (0.560) [1.19]
Average prime lending rate (1-year lag)	$6,541 (29561) [0.22]	– $192,067 (26562) [– 7.23]***	– $53,264 (19166) [– 2.78]*	– $146,411 (41620) [– 3.52]	$ 211 (2726) [0.08]	– $36,712 (9526) [– 3.85]**
Annual no. of growth control measures (3-year lag)	– $18,145 (64074)	– $124,640 (57572)	– $34,826 (53846)	– $21,243 (116928)	– $7,536 (6399)	$36,175 (22362)
Durbin-Watson d	1.26 inc.	1.44 inc.	1.70 inc.	1.34 inc.	1.79 inc.	1.02 inc.

Notes:
* $p < 0.05$
** $p < 0.01$
*** $p < 0.001$
ns   p not significant
inc. d is inconclusive

Table E-2 (continued)

Los Angeles Metropolitan Area (continued)

	Regression coefficient (Standard error) $[t]^p$			
Variable	Riverside		San Bernardino	
	Model 1 $(R^2=0.90)$	Model 2 $(R^2=0.91)$	Model 1 $(R^2=0.96)$	Model 2 $(R^2=0.70)$
Intercept	− $437,336	− $879,866	− $359,331	− $187,349
Population (no lag)	$1.353 (0.14) [9.45]***	$3.978 (0.611) [6.51]***	$0.954 (0.08) [11.75]***	$1.594 (0.65) [2.47]*
Average prime lending rate (1-year lag)	− $6,380 (4609) [− 1.38]	− $91,077 (19655) [− 4.63]***	− $11,734 (3501) [− 3.35]**	− $35,790 (27890) [− 1.28]
Annual no. of growth control measures (3-year lag)	− $41,040 (12603) [− 3.26]**	$57,383 (53748) [1.07]	$14,341 (12231) [1.17]	$122,665 (97434) [1.26]
Durbin-Watson d	2.77 ns	2.34 ns	2.09 ns	1.26 inc.

II. San Francisco Bay Area

Variable	San Francisco		Alameda		San Mateo	
	Model 1 $(R^2=0.48)$	Model 2 $(R^2=0.26)$	Model 1 $(R^2=0.51)$	Model 2 $(R^2=0.58)$	Model 1 $(R^2=0.56)$	Model 2 $(R^2=0.72)$
Intercept	− $683,697	− $589,687	$1,483,763	− $2,096,576	− $1,893,141	$258,960
Population (no lag)	$1.222 (2.28) [0.54]	$1.261 (0.72) [1.75]	$1.602 (0.57) [2.80]*	$2.454 (0.68) [3.60]**	$3.572 (0.98) [3.63]**	$0.530 (1.10) [0.48]
Average prime lending rate (1-year lag)	$42,591 (12891) [3.30]**	− $3,972 (4076) [− 0.97]	$12,304 (7282) [1.69]	− $11,746 (0.68) [− 1.35]	$3,599 (3652) [0.99]	− $22,639 (4088) [− 5.54]***
Annual no. of growth control measures (3-year lag)	$62,544 (148,323) [0.42]	− $1,025 (46901) [− 0.02]	$38,384 (46481) [0.83]	$26,279 (55350) [0.47]	− $17,986 (11180) [− 1.61]	− $6,118 (12516) [− 0.49]
Durbin-Watson d	1.89 ns	2.34 ns	1.90 ns	1.12 ns	1.37 ns	2.48 ns

Table E-2 (continued)

San Francisco Bay Area (continued)

Variable	Regression coefficient (Standard error) [t]^P					
	Santa Clara		Marin		Contra Costa	
	Model 1 (R^2=0.41)	Model 2 (R^2=0.56)	Model 1 (R^2=0.09)	Model 2 (R^2=0.74)	Model 1 (R^2=0.75)	Model 2 (R^2=0.62)
Intercept	– $908,714	– $1,378,670	$65,207	$85,589	– $1,405,852	– $467,845
Population (no lag)	$1.230 (0.64) [1.93]	– $0.206 (0.44) [– 0.47]	$0.021 (1.427) [0.015]	0.831 (1.75) [0.48]	$2.726 (0.53) [5.12]***	$2.183 (0.92) [2.38]*
Average prime lending rate (1-year lag)	$15,289 (15530) [0.98]	– $38,514 (10594) [– 3.64]**	$ 348 (1672) [0.21]	– $11,154 (2045) [– 5.45]***	– $6,339 (6909) [– 0.92]	– $38,909 (11886) [– 3.27]**
Annual no. of growth control measures (3-year lag)	$25,044 (41832) [0.60]	$13,845 (28537) [0.49]	– $9,197 (11627) [– 0.79]	– $19,306 (14223) [– 1.36]	– $155,959 (43307) [– 3.60]**	– $60,543 (74502) [– 0.81]
Durbin-Watson d	1.80 ns	1.62 inc.	1.88 ns	2.91 ns	1.13 inc.	2.17 ns

Variable	Solano		Napa		Santa Cruz	
	Model 1 (R^2=0.16)	Model 2 (R^2=0.73)	Model 1 (R^2=0.05)	Model 2 (R^2=0.54)	Model 1 (R^2=0.44)	Model 2 (R^2=0.37)
Intercept	$248,618	$21,060	$ 714	– $47,691	– $2,294	$168,136
Population (no lag)	– $0.508 (0.47) [– 1.08]	$2.070 (0.503) [4.12]***	$0.493 (0.64) [0.78]	$1.541 (0.68) [2.28]*	$0.239 (0.13) [1.79]	$0.193 (0.33) [0.59]
Average prime lending rate (1-year lag)	– $3,660 (4895) [– 0.75]	– $24,191 (5210) [– 4.64]***	– $ 107 (907) [– 0.12]	– $3,058 (972) [– 3.15]**	$ 537 (1240) [0.43]	– $7,223 (3043) [– 2.37]*
Annual no. of growth control measures (3-year lag)	$7,639 (58769) [0.13]	– $56,983 (62547) [– 0.91]	– $1,853 (4555) [– 0.41]	$2,653 (4877) [0.54]	$5,072 (4321) [1.17]	$9,070 (10608) [0.86]
Durbin-Watson d	2.78 ns	1.93 ns	2.18 ns	1.76 ns	2.04 ns	1.07 ns

Table E-2 (continued)

San Francisco Bay Area (continued)

	Regression coefficient (Standard error) [t]P		
Variable	Sonoma		
	Model 1 (R²=0.12)	Model 2 (R²=0.72)	
Intercept	$23,604	$84,623	
Population (no lag)	$0.363 (0.30) [1.23]	$1.253 (0.35) [3.57]**	
Average prime lending rate (1-year lag)	– $ 291 (3074) [– 0.09]	– $16,301 (3656) [– 4.46]***	
Annual no. of growth control measures (3-year lag)	– $1,207 (13340) [– 0.09]	– $9,265 (15865) [– 0.58]	
Durbin-Watson d	1.49 inc.	2.16 ns	